You'll Never Walk Alone

An autobiography

Canon Harry Sutton

Best wishes
Harry Sutton

Marshalls

Marshalls Paperbacks
Marshall Morgan & Scott
3 Beggarwood Lane, Basingstoke, Hants, RG23 7LP, UK

First published by Marshall Morgan & Scott Ltd.

ISBN 0 551 01148 3

Typeset by Brian Robinson, North Marston, Bucks.

Printed in Great Britain by
Hunt Barnard Printing Ltd., Aylesbury, Bucks.

Contents

This book is dedicated to my wife Olive
who has so selflessly shared the walk with me.

Preface

When it was first suggested that I should share with others the way in which God has dealt with me throughout my life, I hesitated for a long time. It is no secret that whilst I may be able to communicate verbally, I become less effective when I try to put my thoughts and experiences into writing. If therefore I was to write my autobiography it could only be with help.

So it was that I asked my friend of many years standing, Wendy Mann, if she would help me. For more than two decades Wendy has edited and corrected my articles for magazines and religious periodicals so she knows my style well. I was delighted when Wendy consented to cooperate with me in the writing of *You'll Never Walk Alone*. The project would never have come to fruition without her help.

Now that the book is complete, our hope and prayer is that those who read it may, above all, be encouraged. The book does not attempt to catalogue every event in my life and I have not been able to mention so many dear friends who are very important to me. Above all I have tried to introduce the reader to our Lord Jesus Christ whose promise to his believing followers, 'I will be with you always', can be as real today as it was to those to whom the promise was first made. If you claim that promise, you can be assured, 'You'll never walk alone.'

Foreword

I am pleased to write a foreword to Canon Harry Sutton's autobiography. During forty years our lives have touched in significant ways in what were three crossroads, or places of choices for us both.

During the second world war, when the St. John's College was bombed, in order to finish my GOE examination, I transferred to Bristol and met Harry Sutton as a theological student. We both had voices, and were together in a team visiting hospitals singing many a duet.

After completing my exams, I 'threw' a farewell party in my rooms, asking all invitees to come in clerical dress. Harry came as a monk, complete with bare feet, which betrayed him when the Principal came to investigate the noise and found his feet protruding from under my bed!

The late 'fifties' brought the next crossroad in our careers. After returning to London from Chile, South America, I had been nursing the fortunes of the South American Missionary Society along with my parish, which was very close to the Society's offices. During the years that followed, I think we had not only recovered its Founder's dreams for South America, but begun to expand the work, despite the problems of post-war Britain. In addition, we were virtually denied much of the official support of the Anglican Church and South America was rapidly becoming a changing society, industrially and politically, with SAMS still heavily committed in its work amongst the Indians.

Harry Sutton had been doing a vigorous and successful work in a Blackpool Parish, and in 1959 agreed to resign and took over the General Secretaryship of SAMS in 1960 after my consecration as Bishop. He made many visits to South America and must have been a great comfort and cheer to the Mission stations. Under Harry Sutton and a very sound supporting committee, the society went from strength to strength. It was a time when the Society had re-established its purpose and plan for the future and was poised for the big leap forward which Harry so ably led for the next 20 years.

Our next crossroads experience was in 1978 when, retiring from St. Paul's, Portman Square, London, he once again 'stepped into my shoes' and became Vicar. He had not changed since his student days – his humour, exuberance and optimism enlivens all his work for the Master. But not without the cost of depleting his strength and vitality. The unbeliever must bear his cross alone, the Christian must make his cross bear fruit. This he has learned to do, learning the secret of laying hold of Christ's strength when life was not easy, and in that strength to turn its hardness into the sweet fruit of abundant living, making this life not only possible, but full of possibilities.

What follows in this book is the story of one who allowed Christ not only to save his soul, but to change his surroundings.

Bishop A. W. Goodwin-Hudson
(Hon. Assistant Bishop of Derby)
8th July 1984

1: Hello World

'Henry Sutton.' At last the Master of Ceremonies called my name. I'd been waiting with butterflies in my stomach for what seemed an eternity. Now I stepped forward proudly to meet the Queen.

The date was October 24, 1966. The occasion was the opening of the splendid new headquarters of the Church Missionary Society in London's Waterloo Road. Several smaller missionary societies nestled comfortably in the huge building and mine, the South American Missionary Society, was one of them. Canon John V. Taylor, then C.M.S. General Secretary, later Bishop of Winchester, in a characteristically gracious gesture, had invited the General Secretaries of all the societies to meet Her Majesty.

As we assembled in an ante room beforehand, we felt extremely nervous. But we were urged by the Queen's aide to relax. 'Her Majesty will be feeling quite as nervous as you,' we were told!

It was all over in a few moments, but reflecting later I thought how marvellously the Lord had led me to such a privileged occasion. It had all started fifty years earlier in a tiny terraced house in Liverpool: 10, Ogwen Street.

I was born towards the middle of World War One, at the time Sir Douglas Haig was reporting back from the front, 'Rain is supreme and the mud is holding us up.' Young men were setting off daily for France; hundreds of thousands were never to return of course, among them was my brother James who was killed in action shortly after my birth.

On a much less serious note, for years afterwards my mother always enjoyed telling the story of the gypsy who called at our house on the morning of November 25, 1916. The gypsy was there to sell clothes pegs but, seeing a pregnant woman open the door, she couldn't resist telling her fortune: 'The baby will be born later today and it will be a boy.' My mother, who always responded quickly to a bit of fun, pointed out that, as she already had four sons, she was hoping number five might be a girl. Not at all put off, the gypsy insisted that her fifth boy would more than compensate her for the lack of a daughter. She was quickly proved right on the first count: I arrived that afternoon! Then, as the years went by, time proved the second prediction was true too. I was able to compensate my mother in ways that are usually more associated with a daughter. But more of that later.

10, Ogwen Street was one of a monotonous row of eighty four terraced houses. Inside however it was very special, furnished with love. My mother, who had been twenty when James was born, was forty-one by the time I came on the scene. As a child it intrigued me that my parents, Tessie and Bill, got on so well together: they seemed so very different. Mother was short, amply rounded and curved. Father was tall, straight and thin as a beanpole. My mother was a Shimmen, born and bred in the Isle of Man. She mirrored that culture very strongly: volatile and extrovert, packed with energy and devoted to good works. My father, a Staffordshire man, was quiet and retiring. He seldom spoke unless spoken to, and usually kept his feelings to himself. She revelled in meeting people. He like nothing better than to sit with a newspaper or a book. As youngsters they had worked enthusiastically for the Temperance Movement; in fact they met while sharing a platform at a meeting. Now they seemed not at all alike, but I learned of course that often the finest marriages are between a man and a woman who complement rather than duplicate each other.

Then there were my brothers. Leonard was eleven when I was born; William was about to set off as an Infantryman to France; Joseph was an adopted son who served in the Merchant Navy and was old enough to be my father, and James.

We were very much a working class family but I put strong emphasis on 'working'. We lived at the top of Everton Hill, not exactly well off, but rich compared to the families at the bottom of the hill. They knew real poverty and hardship. Unemployment was high and, without any sort of social benefits, families suffered terribly. Children wandered the streets barefoot and hungry, and in some of the back-to-back houses one courtyard toilet had to serve as many as eight families.

My father was one of the fortunate ones: he had a job. He worked for a small firm, Baldock and Co., as a French Polisher. In fact he was foreman. Those were days when Liverpool Docks were alive with men and ships, not like today silent as the grave, and one of Baldock's jobs was to 'touch up' the ships of the famous Blue Funnel and Bibby Line when they eased into the docks for a refit. Sometimes, on a Saturday morning, Dad would show me over one of the ships, and later from the promenade at New Brighton I watched the ships go by and tried to spot 'mine'.

Inside the ships the woodwork – especially the mahogany – shone and gleamed once my father and his men had worked on it. French polishing at that time was a work of art. It was invariably done by hand and I think my father would take unkindly to seeing polish sprayed on to the wood in today's labour-saving environment! Once the wood was stripped, layer upon layer of polish was applied until it shone rock hard and beautiful, bringing out the natural splendour of the grain. My father claimed that, once he had finished a job, you could safely set a hot kettle on the surface without marking it. I am sure it wasn't a vain boast.

Not surprisingly with parents like mine, the inside of 10, Ogwen Street gleamed no less brightly than the mahogany staircases of those great ships. If I close my eyes I can see the little house as clearly as though I lived in it still. It was a basic two rooms down and two rooms up, with a tiny bedroom tucked away at the back (which was to become very precious to me), a little pocket handkerchief of a garden enclosed by forbidding black railings, and the toilet an 'inconvenience' at the far end of the back yard. Home!

Special to me was the parlour, the front room, the best room, reserved for guests and special occasions, and a true illustration of the style of the Edwardian era. It was special because of the open grate which gleamed to elegant perfection; the piano around which we sang to celebrate family reunions; the unique scent of the horse-hair three piece suite and the sparkling mahogany table on which flourished the family aspidistra. It was special finally because the parlour spoke to me of family security, concern and love.

Actually, that aspidistra almost brought my parents to blows – every Christmas! Mother cosseted the plant almost as tenderly as she did her husband and sons, so she was never likely to take kindly to Father's habit of treating its pot as an ash tray for his regular Christmas treat, a Burmese cheroot. To add insult to injury, he even insisted that ash was an excellent fertiliser! Mother huffed and puffed, but the evidence favoured Father because the aspidistra thrived!

Ours was a close knit community. It was a mixed one too. Across the street lived a Polish Jew, Sidney Crossman, and his family. He was a leather worker and I can still smell the pungent scent of the dyes on his tough, leather apron. Next door was an Irish Catholic family called Toal. I recall that at the end of their hall, facing you when the front door opened, was a huge picture of the Sacred Heart, pierced. It terrified me! Further up the street was the postman Jack Rummens and the policeman Billy Mahan. Jack's son was one of my earliest friends but we were not close to the Mahans. This was because my mother viewed all policemen with suspicion. She used to say they would lock up their own grandmothers if it suited them! 84, Ogwen Street was a general store looked after by three delightful ladies. It was always stacked from floor to ceiling with goods ranging from delicious boiled ham to candles and shoe laces.

We had our share of lonely people too. Amy Bott was one of them. She lived alone and the only way she knew of drawing attention to herself was to faint regularly. I think she fainted once a week. The ladies of the street never failed to rush to her aid though.

It was a close knit community. It had to be in order to survive. The National Health Service was a long way off and medical aid was very expensive, so it was essential that everybody pulled their weight in time of need. Mother, for example, proved to be an able midwife and, without any training, was responsible for the safe arrival of many of Ogwen Street's babies.

Our neighbourhood had two focal points: the pub and the church. The pub was the Grapes Hotel, renowned for its hospitality and beer, but even more popular for the landlord's three lovely daughters. It was the ambition of every boy in Ogwen Street at some time or another, to court – and perhaps to catch – one of the delicious Miss Hetheringtons!

But it was Emmanuel Church that claimed my parents' time and interest. Like so many of our neighbours, they were 'religious', loyal churchgoers who would not dream of missing Sunday worship but who did not make the Bible central in their lives or worship. They believed in prayer though and one or other of them never tucked me up in bed at night without uttering the childish prayer:

> Gentle Jesus meek and mild,
> Look upon this little child.
> Pity my simplicity.
> Suffer me to come to Thee.

It meant a lot to me. I never had difficulty in believing in a God who heard our prayers. I never felt alone. I knew God was there.

Each Sunday I very happily accompanied my parents to Emmanuel Church. Canon Arthur Gore Bernard was the minister, a tall and handsome man with distinguished silver hair, inevitably dressed in a frock tail coat. I was too young to sense the possibility then, but the day would come when Canon Bernard would play a significant role in my life. Micky often came too – and he slept throughout the service, usually under a pew. He was another member of the Sutton family, a brown and faithful Irish terrier who shared the first seventeen years of my life. Micky was a favourite dog in the neighbourhood.

One day my parents responded to a call for help from the other end of town. St. Timothy's was what would be known today as a 'downtown' church, rooted firmly at the bottom of Everton Hill, and with few signs of life. A curate with a far from 'downtown' name, the Rev. Garnett Parker Newby, was sent to 'revive the church' and, in true apostolic tradition twelve members of Emmanuel's healthy congregation went to help him.

Because of the long walk to St. Timothy's I still worshipped at Emmanuel, but on church festivals it was considered a special treat to accompany my parents. My father became a churchwarden and along with that responsibility came the privilege of sitting in a pew fitted with a gas lamp. It was a dubious privilege! Services were punctuated with muffled explosions from the lamp, and on each occasion a puff of evil smelling smoke escaped into the atmosphere. I sometimes think that, if the services had been longer than they were, the Suttons might have been gassed during worship!

So, I was a regular and willing churchgoer from the tenderest age. As a very small child I remember looking up at my dad, his finely waxed moustache twitching, as he sang his favourite hymn:

Ten thousand times ten thousand,
In sparkling raiment bright,
The armies of the ransomed saints
Throng up the steeps of light.

Something inside me responded positively to the joyful words – and even today I associate Sunday with the smell of wax!

But, at the age of five, my Mum and Dad were to share my adoration with another lady, Miss Shoe. I fell head over heels in love with her at very first sight.

2: Happy Days

It was my first day at school and, in common with most other girls and boys coming to that first critical point in their lives, I trembled before an unknown future. On that September morning in 1921 my mother helped me into a brown suit I had watched her knitting. I held her hand a little more tightly than usual as we made our way to the rather formidable building that was Steers Street Council School. But once I was handed over to the protective custody of Miss Shoe, all the fears simply drained away. It was love at first sight.

The first morning hurried by in no time and I returned happily home for lunch. There were no school meals in those days, of course. In today's health conscious age, dieticians would probably frown on my regular lunch-time meal which comprised either a jam buttie followed by fruit and a cup of tea, or a condensed milk buttie followed by fruit and a cup of tea! I loved it.

My mother promised me a penny if I was 'a good boy' that first morning. That was no problem with Miss Shoe in charge! I got my penny. On the way back to school I used it to buy three pineapple chunks and three aniseed balls. Back in the classroom Miss Shoe was eagerly offered a sweet from my crumpled bag. I can still recall the extreme pleasure it gave me when my heroine smilingly accepted my sticky offering.

I was no scholar, but I enjoyed school and worked as hard as I could within my capabilities. I wanted to please my parents, I wanted to impress Miss Shoe and I wanted to emulate our headmaster Mr. R. Leith Knipe, who was one of Liverpool's greatest sportsmen and predictably won favour among all the boys. He was quite a character. He cycled to school each day, crouched low, his Edwardian beard brushing the handlebars, a flat cap on his head and a Sherlock Holmes pipe in his mouth.

Miss Shoe was not the only reason for those early schooldays not proving as traumatic for me as they were for some. Going along to Sunday School at Emmanuel Church had prepared me to some extent for being away from home and for something of the discipline too. Judged by today's standards Emmanuel's Sunday School would come well down the bottom of the league, but the place was always crowded out. When we broke up into groups for Bible stories it was almost impossible to concentrate on what our own teacher was saying because of the competition all around us. The hymns and choruses were old fashioned even for those days – 'When He cometh, when He cometh to make up His jewels, precious jewels,' and there was no such thing as a visual aid which we tend to have in excess today. Added to which the premises were dingy, untidy and unattractive.

So what held our attention and drew us to go Sunday after Sunday? It could only have been the teachers themselves. It wasn't so much what they said, it was what they *were* – good and faithful men and women who impressed us with their perseverance and humour and who so clearly believed in what they taught. Victoria Kirk, Elizabeth Lock, May Heath, Mr. Scafe the Superintendent – I remember them all. Hard pressed Sunday School teachers of today, take heart from their example. Be faithful to the Lord and you never know what impression you are making on your inattentive young charges! Remember – today's Sunday School makes tomorrow's Church!

There were two outstanding highlights to the Sunday School year. The first was the Sunday School Anniversary every June. We rehearsed for this for weeks beforehand and it was the ambition of every child to be chosen either to sing or to act. On the great day itself, the children and members of Emmanuel gathered at 2 o'clock ready to parade round the parish before returning to the church for the service at 3 p.m.

Banners waved aloft in the procession. The Church Lads' Brigade and the Scouts carried their banners as did the Church of England Men's Society and the Mothers' Union. At the corner of each street a sizeable crowd gathered to watch and to identify themselves with the church on that day. The clergy as they passed received loud applause. Many of the bystanders joined the procession so that, by the time we returned to the church, the service was filled to capacity.

The other highlight was the annual Sunday School treat, a glorious family day out. We usually went across the Mersey by boat and then by train to Barnston in the Wirral Peninsula. There we spent the day in a large field with a spacious shed, a mat slide and a roundabout. As far as I was concerned it was heaven on earth.

The climax of the day was the Annual Sports. I never won a race on my own but there was a splendid victory with my father in the three-legged. If we had won the Grand National I could not have been more pleased, although the prize was no more than a small bar of chocolate.

Emmanuel did not run a midweek activity for children. Instead, every Tuesday evening, I joined about 30 children in Fabius Baptist Church, a tiny building on the corner of Everton Road and West Derby Road. It was a grey building among many grey buildings, in marked contrast to the colourful Grants Gardens opposite. The gardens had once been a cemetery and my mother told me that tram conductors took great pleasure in calling out, 'All out here for Grants Gardens . . . City of the dead . . . The dead centre of Liverpool.'

There was nothing dead about the children's midweek service in the Baptist church, however. We learned more about Jesus, sang all the evergreen choruses – 'Jesus died for all the children, All the children of the world,' – and, what would certainly set it apart from similar meetings today, heard the temperance cause expounded with passion. I saw the sense of that cause then, and I see the sense of it now – with double the urgency perhaps. I know many Christians would take issue with me, but I find it difficult to understand how Christians can be anything less than advocates of total abstinence. I make that comment in the light of the fact that in England today there are half a million registered alcoholics and at least another half a million unregistered. I think that is total justification of my position. I personally have yet to find a drink more satisfying than tea!

But life wasn't all school and church. Football played a generous part because I had been born into a home of fanatical Liverpool supporters. My father never missed a Saturday afternoon at Anfield Road. The rivalry between Liverpool and Everton was just as intense then as it is today. Dad would rather see Liverpool's fourth team play at Anfield than walk the 600 yards to see Everton's first team playing at Goodison Park!

When I was very small he took me to reserve matches, but once able to cope with the crush of first division crowds, I soon found myself cheering alongside my father and 30,000 other spectators in the terraces of the Kop. There was no roof over our heads as there is today, so it could be perishing cold or soaking wet. But we didn't notice! For about fifteen years the Saturday pattern never changed: roast pork, chips, rice pudding and a cup of tea for lunch; the match itself, then home to – more tea!

My mother years later told me that as she waved us goodbye after Saturday lunch, she had one prayer uppermost in her mind – that my father would come home with his glasses. On a couple of occasions, out of excitement or frustration during a match, he had ripped off his glasses and hurled them into the air! Glasses were not inexpensive in those days and my practical mother failed to appreciate how a football club was worthy of such a sacrifice. Usually however my father's enthusiasm was restrained to singing and cheering – still a marked change of character from the man who, during the week, liked nothing more than a quiet room and a newspaper.

One point I should like to make is that hooliganism at football matches was almost unknown; if it had been otherwise, my father would never have allowed me to go. Aged seven or eight I could be crushed inside the Kop with 30,000 supporters and feel absolutely safe. Unemployment with its attendant emotions of disappointment and frustration was as common in the 1920s as it is in the 1980s, so I am not one who believes that unemployment is an excuse or, as some would go so far as to say, a reason for violence on or off the football pitch. I believe rather that it is more to do with the spirit of the age.

What happened on the football pitch probably helped too. It was a game played with talent and flair, a lot of individualism and good sportsmanship, with all the emphasis on attack and goals. Creativity wasn't stifled as it is today by too much coaching and training. There were no huge contracts or media induced superstars.

As a teenager I played football as well as watched it. I was goalkeeper for Steers Street Council School, a successful team which played in almost every public park in Liverpool during the course of a season. We were called the Bees because of our yellow and black striped jerseys and we were recognised as one of the ablest school teams in Lancashire. Scouts from professional clubs often watched us and I had several trials for Liverpool Schoolboy teams. My father turned up to watch whenever he could and used to stand behind my goal shouting advice. I used to put my mistakes down to his distractions!

We were always a family of familiarity: we had a routine and we kept to it. Mondays for this, Thursdays for that, the Suttons' way of doing things, but it never became boring. I loved each activity for what it was and I revelled in the security of familiar ways. On Sundays, if my voice held up after the shouting the previous afternoon, I sang in Emmanuel's choir. We dressed in cassocks, surplices, Eton collars and Dicky bows – the works! I belonged to Wolf Cubs and later Scouts. On Tuesdays, as I grew older, I seldom missed a visit to the Olympia Picture House – and fell in love again, this time with every schoolboy's idol, Janet Gaynor. On Thursdays I queued outside the Hippodrome Theatre for cheap gallery seats and, standing outside the stage door, brushed shoulders with the stars as they arrived – Gracie Fields, Nellie Wallace, Randolph Sutton, George Formby and many other great entertainers. Friday night was choir practice. It was all routine, but it was a routine which offered broad and varied experience so that I felt life was full and stimulating.

I first joined the church choir at the age of eight and after a year or two I was promoted along with Billy McGill to being a 'back leader'. This simply meant that we led the choir into the vestry when the service was over. Billy was a swarthy boy with a shock of jet black hair. I, in contrast, was extremely fair. This led to us being given the nicknames 'Cherubim and Seraphim'. Even today I cannot return to West Derby Road without some of the elderly residents addressing me as 'Cherubim'!

The Wolf Cubs deserved my loyalty: being a member gave me nothing but pleasure. Later I progressed to the 144th Liverpool Scout Troop and loved to yell with the others:

> Who's the best troop in the East?
> Who ah? The 1 4 4!

Football competitions, swimming galas, athletics, camp, our life together reverberated with fun and noise. Our band, I remember, comprised eight Cavalry B Flat trumpets, four drums and a bass drum. The trumpets always got the better of us and the art of marching in time while playing quite escaped us. The Church Lads' Brigade, with military style discipline were, on the other hand, magnificent on parade. Once, in order to show the Brigade that we knew a thing or two as well, we tried some unrehearsed countermarching, only to finish up in an undignified and hysterical heap in the middle of the high street!

After a couple of years as a Cub I was promoted to the coveted position of a Sixer which made me responsible for looking after five younger Cubs in the pack. Norman Cowden, a leading Scout in the county of Lancashire, was the man behind the Scout Troop and I shall always be grateful to him for that promotion. I can still feel myself bristling with pride as he greeted me with a customary, 'Hallo Squire!' Being a Sixer provided me with an early taste of leadership, its problems as well as its privileges, which stood me in good stead later in life.

Progression into the Scout movement brought a new pleasure as I became a member of the Rip Raps, the Scout troop concert party. Its standard was always first class. For my first ever solo with the Rip Raps I was dressed in cricket whites with a red scarf round my neck and a black wig perched on my head. My face and hands were darkened with burnt cork – for this was the Black and White Minstrel Show! I remember the song:

Walking in a Winter wonderland,
Down the lane; sleigh bells ringing.

I practised for weeks and put all I had into singing it well.

Pantomime was an important part of the Rip Raps' repertoire. I played an Ugly Sister in Cinderella one year and the Mad Hatter in Alice in Wonderland another. It was great fun and it also gave me the confidence to stand in front of a large audience and taught me how to hold them. I sensed how much I enjoyed this and it proved a valuable lesson for the future. I didn't, of course, realise this fact at the time, nor did I have any inkling that the most significant event of my life was to take place a few years later through the influence of a Scout leader and friend called John O'Brien.

One last reference to familiar ways – and my story would not be complete without it – is Christmas. I don't think the Sutton family ritual at Christmas changed at all for twenty years. It really began for me when I collected my mother's bread and bun loaves from the baker's. She was a splendid cook – her pancakes and potato cakes were superb – but her scope was limited by an oven which, heated only by an open fire at one side, could not be regulated with any accuracy. So it was only at Christmas that she made bread and it was my responsibility to carry it to the local bakery for cooking. Hours later I returned to fetch it. The yeasty aroma from the warm bread in the crisp cold of a late December afternoon was exquisite. I knew that Christmas had arrived.

The next thrill was to hang up my stocking at the end of my bed every Christmas Eve. It bulged attractively in the morning and I was never disappointed with what I found. I don't think I ever had more than two main presents, but that was all I expected and all I wanted. Also, it was all my parents could afford. Some children today seem to have as much as a hundred pounds or more spent on them, but in those less sophisticated days a few shillings ensured a happy Christmas for a child. Two favourite gifts stand out in my memory: a pedal car which travelled many miles up and down Ogwen Street, and a fort and toy soldiers bought for the princely sum of two shillings and sixpence (about 13 p in today's currency). I knew the price because I had gazed longingly at them through a shop window!

The presents opened, my brothers and their families descended on us. First we all marched off to church for the Carol Service; then came the very traditional Christmas Dinner and after that merriment in the parlour where we played the same games and cracked the same jokes year after year. I was never short of company; my brothers had children of their own and I was an uncle by the age of six – to Alexander my brother William's son. In the evening my mother's dearest friend, Bridget Tudor arrived with her family. Bridget was a devoted Roman Catholic, my mother no less a devout Protestant; not only that but Bridget was the wife of a publican and my mother was still a committed supporter of the Temperance Cause. It could have made for tension and bitterness. Instead, because neither woman had a trace of bigotry or prejudice in her make-up, their strong convictions, however different, gave them respect for each other. So Christmas Day ended with songs round the piano, turkey and ham sandwiches, mince pies and jelly, not forgetting plenty of cups of tea.

On Boxing Day the pattern was reversed and repeated. This time the Suttons descended on the Tudors in their private apartment above the Fitzroy Arms.

In this way my childhood was a happy and stable one.

The church played a major role, but not in any oppressive way. I was always happy within its organisations and among its members. And yet, when I had my first real encounter with God at the age of thirteen, it didn't happen because of the church; it happened because of a memorable gift from my parents – a Rudge Whitworth bicycle which had North Road drop handlebars and cost £4. 19s. 6d.

3: Quest and Conversion

I couldn't wait to try out my gleaming new bicycle. Pedalling furiously I set off at once for my brother William's house about five miles away. The bike was all I hoped it would be and I became thoroughly absorbed in my ride. Suddenly though, I became conscious of the noise and fumes of a huge lorry bearing up on me from behind. My concentration wavered and I careered violently sideways. The next think I knew was lying on a grass verge with the lorry's front wheel shuddering a few inches from my head. I think the lorry driver was even more shaken than I. He jumped down from his cab, uncertain whether or not he had managed to brake in time. 'Phew son!' he exclaimed when he realised I was still in one piece, 'there must be some special angel up there looking after you. It's a miracle you're not dead.'

A very relieved man, he drove off. I was no less relieved to discover that my Rudge Whitworth was still intact! Then it was during those moments afterwards that I distinctly felt the presence of God, felt that I could almost reach out my hand and touch him. He, I realised, had saved me – and saved me for a purpose. I heard Him speak to me: He had a plan for my future and I would know what it was when the right moment came. It was a fleeting experience, but one so significant that it burned deeply into my consciousness; so much so that, although I had many subsequent experiences of the love of God, that one still stands out.

Strangely perhaps my confirmation months later

didn't mean nearly so much to me. That was despite eight weeks of preparation classes and confirmation at the hands of Dr. Gresford Jones, Suffragan Bishop of Warrington, who preached a clear Gospel message. He challenged us to choose or reject Christ, that was the most crucial decision in anyone's life. He was a lovely man. I remember that he had the habit of leaving the pulpit during his sermon and strolling up and down the aisle, which was his way of holding a congregation's attention. I remember too how his face creased into a thousand contented wrinkles as he placed trembling hands on my head. I say it didn't have much influence on me but that may have had something to do with another event looming even nearer and filling my waking and some of my sleeping thoughts . . . leaving school and finding a niche in the working world.

I worked particularly hard during my last year at school; even the headmaster noticed and commented on it. But a willingness to work hard was no guarantee of employment for a fourteen year old. That was when my parents again proved their love for me. At great financial sacrifice they sent me to Fairfield Commercial College. It was most unusual for those of my social class to have the opportunity to go there. The course lasted eighteen months and taught the skills of typing, Pitman's shorthand and elementary book-keeping: skills which have proved very useful over the years. I had only been there for a few months however when my father's employer, John Baldock, died suddenly and his firm went into liquidation. It was a terrible shock – especially to my hard-working father, who found unemployment a frustrating and disappointing experience. There was an unwritten code of practice for unemployed French polishers: they congregated in a dock shed where foremen from firms looking for labour would come and look them over. Dad didn't miss a day, but he was never taken on. He knew why too; most of the foremen were Roman Catholic and he was well known as a staunch and active Protestant. If that sounds too harsh a judgement, perhaps I should add that there were many instances too of Protestants wronging Catholics.

As a child I had always loved to watch the Orange Day parades on July 12. I was deeply impressed by the colour and pageantry, the enthusiasm of the bands and the openness with which the Bible was displayed. This all changed for me because of one particular parade. Two or three bandsmen broke free of the main parade which was wending its way through a predominantly Catholic part of town, grabbed an old zinc bath they found abandoned in the gutter and heaved it through the window of the nearest house. These young Orangemen, visibly impressed with their cleverness, scurried back to their places, leaving behind them an irate and bemused Catholic family. It was no way to start healing relationships; it was no way to reveal the Christ of the Gospels.

I still find myself recalling that incident when I see Protestants and Catholics marching in Northern Ireland. How can they pray to God, read their Bibles and go to church while at the same time they call down destruction on their supposed enemies and are often not above meeting violence with violence? Undoubtedly there exists a negative, sterile, destructive kind of religion which bears no relation whatsoever to the Gospel of Jesus Christ – and we should be prepared to condemn it without reservation.

My father, though out of work, never lost his dignity – nor did many thousands of other men in the same position. Unemployment did not – in the twenties – lead to nearly the same amount of violence on the streets or vandalism as is evident today. Week by week Dad collected his meagre dole and somehow we survived. Years later a friend of mine, who had just been refused permission to marry the girl he loved because the girl's father thought him too poor, protested, 'I'm not poor. The only thing I don't have is money.' I knew just what he meant; it summed up my parents. They were poor in material terms, but rich in everything that really mattered. But my father did not have to endure the dole for too long. He contacted two of his former colleagues at Baldock's and together they managed to scrape up the massive deposit of £100. With this he set up his own French polishing business, Bill Sutton and Co. With hard work it soon went from strength to strength and we were back on our feet again.

College came to an end and now it was my turn to search for a job. I was one among thousands of teenagers for whom the prospects looked bleak, but as it turned out I was one of the few fortunate ones. For that I had to thank Alfred Hodgson, a member of Emmanuel Church who recommended me to his boss. An interview followed and then I found myself a shipping clerk with the West African Drug Company, a subsidiary of R. Sumner and Company, chemists and druggists in Hanover Street, Liverpool. I would have been thankful for almost any job, but in fact I enjoyed what proved to be responsible work. I often visited Liverpool Customs House where I had to declare any articles being exported to West Africa which contained dangerous drugs. I earned 12/6d a week and was promised an annual rise of half a crown. Riches indeed!

Eighteen months into my job I experienced God again, not on my bicycle this time, but in the rather more orthodox surroundings of a church. Church still played a major role in my life. While my father was out of work I had joined in the 'Bishop's Mission', a major evangelistic outreach throughout the diocese of Liverpool. It took my mind off the troubles at home. I attended everything – services, open air meetings and united rallies – but, as yet, there was no personal commitment. There was a change however. I was no longer prepared to accept everything I was told about God. Although I couldn't have put it in such terms, I was becoming more spiritually aware. For example, during that mission there were plenty of opportunities for people to question the missioners and I remember how shocked I was when one missioner calmly assured an enquirer that prayers for the dead were not only permissible but desirable. At 14 I knew nothing about theology. Even today, fifty years on, I am no theologian, but I sensed deep down that the missioner was wrong, seiously wrong; that the Bible contradicted him and that man's eternal destiny is decided only by how he responds *now* to the claims of Christ. I didn't know it at the time, but seeds planted over the years by parents, Sunday School teachers and ministers were beginning to grow and a few to yield fruit.

At this stage of my life, one of my most vivid recollections is of going for a short walk down the road to Canning Dock where ships were being repaired and others were off-loading their cargoes. The smell of the sea and of the tar being used for repairs is one that remains with me still.

In the corner of the dock was a coil of thick rope forming a cylinder. I loved to jump into the coil of rope in search of solitude. Sometimes I prayed. It became a kind of spiritual home; somewhere I could escape for a few moments from the office and the pressures of life; where I could look up, see the clouds scurrying by and feel the presence of a yet partially known God.

As I look back on my life, I cannot think of any more sacred place to me than that coil of rope. I was most certainly not alone. There were times when it was as full of the Holy Spirit as the upper room on the day of Pentecost.

As a sign of further maturity I took up Sunday School teaching. We used as our basis the books for Sunday

School teachers by J.R. Ballein. There were at least twelve such books and each gave ideas for a suitable address for each Sunday of the year. I did not find Sunday School work easy. In fact I still find it difficult to work with small groups. But I took the task seriously and did the best I could. I still have all my J.R. Ballein books and find much in them is still very relevant today.

A real highlight in my life at this time was when Hallelujah Thompson, an Irish Church Army Captain visited us. When he came to your parish in his horse drawn caravan it was your church's responsibility to provide hospitality for the Captain and food and water for his horse! His preaching at Emmanuel could not have been more fiery and urgent and to the point: 'You *must* be born again.' But he was not after easy converts; he was one of the first evangelists I knew who believed in emphasising the cost as well as the privilege of Christian discipleship. He also illustrated his Bible talks with Magic Lantern slides. These were enormous glass sheets with black and white pictures, most of which featured angels and harps! They were terribly old fashioned – but this was the 1930s and to me the Magic Lantern was nothing short of sensational.

Teenagers, in fact, flocked to hear Hallelujah Thompson. There was something special about the man, not least his gentle Irish humour. Every year when he returned to his native Ireland for a holiday, hundreds of us would be found on the Liverpool docks landing stage, singing hymns and choruses and waving an affectionate farewell.

But still I had not fully responded to the Gospel message. There was however soon to be a further memorable, personal encounter with God culminating in my own new birth. I had read about it, talked about it, seen it happen to others, listened to ministers proclaim it, but only now was it to become heart knowledge rather than head knowledge; only now was

Christ going to transform *my* life and not just the lives of people I knew. It began and ended with a powerful but straightforward evangelistic sermon, the type I had heard hundreds of times in the past, but which only now – in God's perfect timing – was going to get through to *me*.

The final stages in my spiritual journey to Christ and the 'new birth' did not begin at Emmanuel but at a mission church in the next parish. This was during the period after mission churches had sprung up all over working class areas. The reason for them only cast a sad reflection on the Church of England. Putting it bluntly, working class Christians felt uncomfortable and out of place in a typical parish church. Even worse, those in shabby clothes who had a poor life style, probably through no fault of their own, were not made welcome in the main church. Today, of course, the Church of England is reaping what it sowed and still finds it difficult to throw off its predominantly middle class image and appeal.

It was the mission church attached to St. Chrysostom in Everton that attracted me to its midweek harvest service. The Vicar was the Rev. Russell White, later to become Bishop of Tonbridge, but that night the preacher was his curate the Rev. Maurice Garner who, I am happy to report, is still alive and well and living in Weymouth. He preached from the text Jeremiah 8 v. 20: 'The harvest is past, the summer is ended, and we are not saved.' Again, as on that grass verge after the accident, I heard God challenge me: '*You* are not saved.' This time I responded: 'But I do want to be saved, Lord.' From that moment I hungered and thirsted for a relationship with Christ, but was unsure how to achieve it. Someone who quite transparently had what I wanted was John O'Brien, Scout leader and friend. He not only testified to a conversion experience, but his life seemed radically different from mine. He talked of God freely and spontaneously; he knew God as a friend and he was conscious of God guiding his life – the daily routine as well as the major, critical decisions.

By now I was eighteen. I was a senior Scout and led the Badger Patrol. Scouting taught us the value of three attributes – self reliance, teamwork and a healthy respect for authority. I sometimes regret that the Scout movement today bears only faint resemblance in numbers or in motivation, to the movement I grew to love. As a Patrol leader I welcomed younger members to call round and have a chat. My mother always treated them to her famous pancakes or potato cakes which were always popular. I thoroughly enjoyed this experience.

One of the highlights of the scouting year was the annual camp and, in 1934, not only were we booked into one of my favourite haunts, Peel on the Isle of Man, but I was to share a tent with John and his best friend. That meant early morning prayers and Bible Study. I found it a trifle embarrassing at first, especially as I had no Bible of my own, but by the end of the week I was finding the Bible irresistible in its appeal. In fact I trace my lifelong love for the Word of God back to that Scout camp.

I returned home dissatisfied and unfulfilled. But not for long. Within a week John, sensing my frustration and need, accompanied me to an evangelistic tent campaign in the centre of Newsham Park. I don't remember the sermon that night, but all that mattered was that the Scottish evangelist invited anyone who longed to commit their life to Christ to come forward for counselling and prayer. I was one of the first to respond!

I was born again that night, unmistakably and gloriously converted. The joy was intense; I was bursting with happiness; my sins were forgiven; Christ ruled my life; I was His and He was mine for ever. A new and adventurous life was beginning and, looking back over fifty years, I can honestly say that I never regretted that first crucial commitment and that, although I have often failed Christ, He has never failed me.

I don't think my feet touched the ground as I walked home. Such was my euphoria that my mother's reaction to the news that I was now a Christian did not affect me at all, 'What on earth have you been all these years then?' She was baffled. The next day was Sunday. I barely drew breath from morning to night as I enthused over my conversion and what it meant. My parents were impressed and needed little persuasion to accompany me back to the campaign the following evening. If anyone had told me on Saturday evening that I could know even greater joy, I would not have believed him, but then I did not know what was to happen on Monday. My beloved mum and dad also committed their lives to Christ.

It was an unforgettable weekend with much to reflect on later. My parents had been regular, fervent churchgoers all their lives, yet they were in their sixties before they encountered the Person behind the Gospel story. I have wondered many times since just how many thousands of churchgoers are in the same position? They know *about* God, but they don't *know* God Himself.

So the Sutton family – or at least father, mother and youngest son – were all born of the Spirit of God within hours of each other and were now united in the goal of following Christ and telling others about Him. As for me, what happened in that tent meant that a new life was mapped out – one I could not have anticipated, one I would not have believed possible.

4: Come Follow . . .

As a new Christian I felt a spontaneous desire to share my new found faith and joy with others. I continued happily as a member of Emmanuel Church but, apart from Sunday School teaching, I realised that the opportunity to express my faith there would be purely by way of personal witness. The rigid structures within the Church of England in those days made it almost impossible for anyone but an ordained minister to speak in the church hall, let alone the church itself.

Today, of course, the structures have eased a little but, in my opinion, not anything like enough. I believe it is because of the restrictions placed upon lay people in the traditional churches that the House Church Movement has flourished in recent years. The traditional churches should have known better. We have only to look back to the Acts of the Apostles to see how essential it is for new Christians to be able to express their faith both verbally and practically. The present House Church Movement became necessary for a number of reasons, not the least being that born again men and women felt stifled and frustrated by church structures. Sadly however we now see appearing in them the very things the Movement came into being to destroy. Excesses now sometimes outweigh the undouted benefits. The Movement particularly reacted against one man ministries, but it now practises the sort of discipleship where one man can totally dominate the lives of others.

I thank God that my need was very soon met. Doors were opened to me that were not opened for everyone. Early on I was introduced to the National Young Life Campaign and this was to have the most significant outcome. Not only did my spiritual life thrive within the N.Y.L.C. but my emotional life too. A girl called Olive entered my life . . . and never left it!

It all began the August Bank Holiday Monday after my conversion. I was invited to spend the day with members of the Merseyside N.Y.L.C. We met at Liverpool's Lime Street Station where I was astonished to find, not the fifty young people I had expected, but about four hundred. There were many more Christians around that I had supposed! Our destination was Overton Hills in Cheshire where we began a ramble through the countryside until we reached the noted beauty spot of Delamere. There we had tea and then held an open air service before making the return journey. It was a tea that changed my life! I could not take my eyes off the girl behind the tea urn! There she stood, smiling and chatting as she filled our cups. I discovered that her name was Margaret Olive Rourke and that she liked to be called Olive. But that was as far as things went that day. I was too nervous and too new on the scene to try to make further conversation.

However during the meal I was asked if I had heard someone called Gavin Hamilton preach. I hadn't so much as heard of Mr. Hamilton. Apparently he was a Brethren evangelist currently conducting a tent campaign in Rock Ferry on the Cheshire side of the Mersey. 'Come along and hear him next Saturday,' I was urged. I didn't need persuading: Olive might be there . . .!

It was work as usual the following week but my mind was not always on the job. There was Olive to think about. So intense were my thoughts about her as Saturday approached that they turned into a kind of prayer – a very simple and self-centred prayer admittedly. It was along the lines of asking God to make sure Olive was at Rock Ferry, even if all the others who had said they would be there couldn't make it.

That Saturday evening I arrived at the Liverpool landing stage in very good time. The paddle steamer called Ruby was nowhere to be seen; nor were my new friends; nor was Olive. Then they began to arrive in ones and twos and I greeted them rather off-handedly, peering over their heads for someone else. Then – there she was . . . looking a picture, dressed in a close-fitting, light grey, pin-striped coat, with a Robin Hood style hat to match. I felt as though I would gladly have swum up the river just to be with Olive for the evening, but that was not necessary, we got on the ferry boat together! I think I remembered to breathe a quick 'Thank You' to God.

I found out that evening that Olive was a children's nurse. She worshipped at Oakdale Presbyterian Mission in Wallesey where she had become a Christian. Her home was a Christian one, but it was clear that she had been brought up in a much stricter atmosphere than I had been. Olive's father had been a sea-captain until she was twelve, and then replaced the sea with the land by becoming a Salvation Army officer. However Olive's parents were both now dead – as indeed was one of her brothers – so she and another younger brother were quite alone in the world. I decided I wanted to change all that!

If the N.Y.L.C. had proved its worth by introducing me to Olive, it also played a vital role in toughening me up as a Christian, disciplining me and opening up opportunities to serve the Lord. I attended their meetings and rallies as often as I could, and soon came to know the staff. It was not long before I was asked to give my testimony at meetings led by an outstanding evangelist of the day, Stanley Phillips. He had been a missionary in Brazil and was now the N.Y.L.C. evangelist for the North West.

Perhaps the *most* outstanding evangelists of the time were Frederick, Arthur and Harding Wood – the Wood brothers – who had founded the N.Y.L.C. and could be found evangelising young people all over the country. One day they asked me to accompany them on a local campaign and to give my testimony. I was one of several given this honour in the presence of the newly appointed staff evangelist, a young Roy Hession who was later renowned as the author of the spiritual classic, 'The Calvary Road'.

I think it was during that meeting, in a packed hall in Rochdale, that I acquired an enthusiasm for mass evangelism that has never left me. I was very nervous before I stood up, but afterwards, as I watched young people come forward to commit their lives to Christ, I vowed I would never miss an opportunity to tell others of my faith. Just one convert would make all the nerves worthwhile.

The Wood Brothers had a major influence on my Christian life. As well as being powerful evangelists, they were fervent advocates of the need for Christians to be 'separate from the world'. Frederick Wood even wrote a book called, 'Questionable Amusements'. Some thought they were too extreme in the standards they set for new converts, but as I studied the Bible I found that they were only setting out *Christ's* standards.

I believe that this whole issue of separation – being *in* the world but not *of* it, being markedly different from non-Christians, without of course becoming exclusive or superior – is one that today's Church should examine closely in the presence of God. All too often, it seems to me, Christians merge ineffectively into the activities and, worse still, the spirit of the world. There is all too little evidence of what Christ commanded us to be – lights shining on a hill, salt cleansing and preserving society.

A new friend I made after my conversion was Albert Croft. He, his father and brother were fine preachers and, although they were unable to practise their gift in the Anglican Church, they often preached in nonconformist churches. They were very popular too. It was about a year after my conversion that Albert asked if I could deputise for him the following Sunday in a little mission hall off West Derby Road. Growing in confidence and increasing – just a little – in Bible knowledge, I agreed to help. The mission halls had an atmosphere of their own: a kind of cosy spirituality inside and a militant evangelistic spirit outside.

So it was that about forty people heard my first Gospel message on 'Life's Greatest Question – What Shall I Do With Jesus Who Is Called Christ?' (Pilate's words from Matthew 27 v. 22). I could not have fared too badly because afterwards my name was passed to an elderly couple who looked after the Chester Street Mission in Birkenhead. I preached there too – I think I managed a different sermon! – and was not at all put off by the fact that the hall had once been a butcher's shop!

I have two outstanding recollections of my first visit to the Chester Street Mission. There was a huge boiler in the room and it was the lot of the preacher to sit right next to the boiler for the first part of the service. I had almost melted by the time I was called upon to speak! I gratefully rose to my feet and edged as far away from the boiler as I could in order to give my address.

The second recollection – and a much more significant one – is that of the elderly gentleman in charge of the mission drawing me aside after the service, placing a hand on my shoulder and saying, 'Young man, I believe God will call you to become an evangelist if you pray hard and work hard.'

His words shook me. I had never so much as contemplated the possibility. A testimony here, a brief

Gospel address there, that was all I thought I was capable of doing. This throwaway remark at the end of the evening ultimately changed my life. For the moment it persuaded me to discuss the possibilities with Olive, whom I was seeing regularly now, and my father.

My father was all for being practical. He wanted to hear me preach before he gave any opinion or advice. He said he would come with me if I was invited to preach again. But my enthusiasm could not wait for invitations – I suggested I would like to try some open air preaching the next week.

So, the next Saturday evening Dad and I made our way to Islington Square, a kind of Hyde Park of its day, where cranks and oddbods, as well as sincere and earnest speakers, were allowed to have their say. Among those who never missed a Saturday were members of the Communist Party, the Independent Labour Party and the Anti-Vivisection League.

I stood on a box and preached while my father stood beside me ready to chat to anyone who seemed interested in what I was saying. It was a strange sensation when people actually stopped to listen to *me*. The little knot of people around my box was quite as big as that around any of the other speakers. There was sometimes heckling and questions from the crowd which I, as a youngster of 19 to 20, found it difficult to handle as well as I would have liked, but I enjoyed the experience. That was to prove the first of many Saturday evenings spent in Islington Square.

Dad used to come with me and hadn't forgotten why. One evening as we walked home together up Brunswick Road, he came out with the question, 'Harry, have you ever thought of going into the Ministry?' That threw me into even more confusion that the Chester Street experience. Dad meant 'the Anglican Ministry' and what chance did I have with so little education and coming from a working class background? Such a question got

Olive and me praying even harder for guidance.

The little upstairs bedroom at 10, Ogwen Street was becoming a very precious and holy place. Night after night I knelt and prayed, studied my Bible, learned more about Christ, worshipped Him and poured out the needs of the people I knew. It was one such night, as I prayed by candlelight, that I became unusually aware of another presence in the room. I *knew* the Lord was there. I sensed it, I gloried in it and I distinctly heard Him calling me to take a step of faith and, putting human fears behind me, to enter His service full time. From that moment I never doubted it was possible. The Lord had sealed His call and, if He was with me, who could be against me? Not until that evening had the hymn meant so much to me:

> I heard the call, 'Come follow,'
> That was all.
> Earth's joys grew dim,
> My soul went after Him.
> Will you not follow if you hear Him call?

My parents were the first to hear the news. My father showed no surprise but, as always, he proved to be the practical one: no head in the clouds for him, not even if it was his son's head and they were spiritual clouds. He advised me to go and talk things over with our Vicar. Canon Bernard did nothing to boost my confidence. I don't mean that as a criticism. He was quite right to point out my lack of academic qualifications and, although he didn't say as much, he probably doubted my aptitude for the kind of study that would be necessary to obtain them. But he *was* impressed by my sense of God's calling and he promised to pray about it. A week later he called on me to say that he too believed God wanted me in the Anglican Ministry.

I now had the support of the people who mattered most to me: my parents, Olive and Canon Bernard. Now it was up to me. Our Vicar stressed the importance of taking one hurdle at a time and the first one standing in my path was clearly labelled 'academic qualifications'. But when God calls He prepares the way. Quite recently Canon Bernard, Canon Lindsey and other Liverpool clergy had established a night school, the Liverpool Evangelical Tutorial School, especially for the purpose of helping young men in my position.

These eminent churchmen had recognised that capable, working class youngsters left school with no formal qualifications simply because of lack of opportunity in the council schools. It was virtually impossible for any working class young man to enter the ministry therefore: he just did not have the most basic qualifications. The new School's aim was simple: to provide the means for obtaining that qualification. And what was so marvellous was that the diocese had agreed that any young man who passed successfully through the School would be seriously considered for the ministry. It was perfect timing as far as I was concerned.

So began the hard slog of studying. And it was a hard slog! Many were the moments when, if there had been any doubt about the validity of God's call, I would have given up. But I knew God had chosen me and I was not going to let Him down. One problem hit me at the outset: in those days, to obtain a Matriculation certificate, one had to pass seven subjects. One failure in seven meant no certificate. And mathematics was one of the seven subjects. Now I knew, my father knew, everyone who watched me through school knew, that if I lived to be a hundred I would never pass mathematics. How thankful I was to discover there was just a little flexibility in the syllabus: I was allowed to replace Maths with Logic. What a relief! I enjoyed Logic and found it relatively straightforward.

From the very beginning, Olive was right alongside me. My studies took up three evenings a week and it was Olive who helped me to discipline myself to work on the other nights too. We still had precious opportunities to be together however, especially as we had discovered a mutual love of music. In fact we became quite well known in local Christian circles for our duets . . . and we visited several of the small mission halls along the Dock Road, revelling in the chance to witness together. One of our favourite songs was:

I am a stranger here,
Heaven is my home

. . . and never were the words more appropriate than when we sang them in the Anchor of Good Hope Public House in Toxteth. It was reckoned to be tough just to drink there, so imagine how we felt appearing to sing Christian hymns! But there was never any trouble. Our witness revealed that people are the same wherever they are, whatever their circumstances: sinful, lonely, searching and in desperate need of a Saviour.

Something else we did together once a year was to join the Children's Special Service Mission (C.S.S.M.) team on holiday at Cleveleys, a seaside resort to the north of Blackpool. Come August, Olive and I could be found enjoying happy Christian fellowship at a boarding house called Aldwyn under the watchful eye of proprietresses Miss Dumble and Miss Sloan – lovely Christian ladies but very old-fashioned! One story will show what I mean.

Some of the girls in our team were spotted on the beach by Miss Dumble – and they were not wearing stockings. Consternation! This was considered a serious lapse into worldliness – not one though, as I recall, mentioned in Frederick Wood's book! This was the subject of discussion and prayer that evening, and either

Miss Sloan or Miss Dumble suggested that our girls wore black stockings to signify their separation from worldly standards. How times change! Black stockings today of course are seen as the very symbol of worldliness! I don't think their extreme advice was carried out, but certainly the girls did not appear barelegged on the beach again – not that year anyway!

The holiday at Cleveleys made a welcome break from working by day at Sumners and by night at Tutorial School. We told children about Jesus, preaching on the beach from a sand pulpit. We organised Bible quizzes and told Bible stories. As we did so, lasting friendships were made. James Seddon, later to become a well known hymn writer, was the leader of our first Cleveleys holiday and many were the times when our paths were to cross in future. One day I would be godfather to his daughter Pat.

Not only was it a welcome break, it also revitalised our Christian witness back home. And as we witnessed so we were nourished by a host of famous preachers who passed through Liverpool: Pastor Edward Jeffries and his brother who were to become founders of the Elim Movement; Lionel B. Fletcher, an exciting evangelist from New Zealand; Harold Wildish, a missionary in the West Indies; Dr. Edwin Orr and John Scroggie. All men to whom I, and many others, owe a great debt of gratitude.

As my period of study at the Liverpool Evangelical Tutorial School drew to a close, I was more and more conscious of the climate in the Church of England. The dividing lines of churchmanship were not so clearly drawn as they are today; there were three distinct types, but the differences lay more in their external forms of worship rather than in any fundamental doctrinal convictions. As far as I could make out – and this was only the considered opinion of a twenty year old – there were high churches, central churches and low churches.

Our church Emmanuel was low: there were no vestments, a minimum of ceremony and we adhered faithfully to the 1662 Prayer Book services. But whether a church was low or high counted for very little as far as its spiritual life was concerned. A low church could be spiritually dead; a high church spiritually vibrant and vice-versa. External show said little about a church's spiritual effectiveness.

However doctrinal differences were becoming more pronounced as a result of a split – in 1922 – within the ranks of the Church Missionary Society. Then there had been concern in some quarters over certain doctrines being taught in CMS colleges overseas. Those who felt strongly about it, in order to safeguard the authority and inspiration and centrality of the Bible, founded a new Society – the Bible Churchmen's Missionary Society.

I did not know it as I came to the end of my Tutorial School studies – but developments within the two societies were to mean a lot to me in the years ahead . . .

5: Preparation for Christian Service

One only had to read the newspaper headlines in the late Thirties to realise that Britain was once more edging towards the brink of war. With the memory of the horrors of World War One still fresh in our minds, we dreaded another war but there seemed nothing to do but simply press on with life's daily tasks and not to think too often about the future. Posing the question, 'If there's a war, what will that mean for my studies and my hopes?' would have been understandable, but also disconcerting.

So life continued. For me this meant obtaining diocesan approval for my dream of ordination into the Anglican ministry. In those days there was no selection board appointed by a central authority; one was interviewed by members of a Diocesan Board of Examiners.

I remember two of these very well: Canon Bezzant, a Residentiary Canon of the Cathedral, and Canon Lomax, a Liverpudlian Vicar. They were two very different men. Canon J. S. Bezzant came from a radical school of thought and his interpretation of the Christian faith would not have matched mine. However he did not ask me one question of a doctrinal nature; instead he seemed intent on discovering my views of and attitudes to the fair sex!

Canon Lomax, on the other hand, was a straightforward evangelical churchman whose questioning concentrated on my conversion and the reality of my call to the ministry. He made sure too that I understood the sacrifices involved in following such a path. He also probed quite deeply into my background and upbringing. He seemed genuinely interested in me as a whole person.

Reports went to a Diocesan Board and I heard soon afterwards that I had been approved and accepted for training. Now came the problem of finance. There were no grants at that time and fees at theological college were about £30 a term. This meant I needed to find £100 from somewhere just to get through the first of my three years. This may not sound much, but this was 1938 remember and I was still earning little more than £1 a week. The Diocesan Board of Finance helped as much as they could: they said that if I could find the £200 necessary to cover two years' fees, they would be prepared to lend me £100 for the third year. There was a sting in the tail however: I was not to get married before – out of my curate's stipend, the loan had been repaid. I had to share that news with Olive of course. I knew perfectly well what her attitude would be: having identified herself with my calling right from the start, she was willing to make any necessary sacrifice to see it come to fruition. She has maintained this same identification now for fifty years and I can never thank God enough for her.

So all I could do was to leave my financial needs with the Lord and go ahead and make preparations for the great move. I decided to join the Bible Churchmen's Missionary and Theological College in Bristol. The rift between CMS and BCMS was still a sensitive issue and my theological sympathies were very much with the new society. The diocese was not too happy with my decision, but they did not stand in my way. Thus, within days, I found myself at BCMS Headquarters in

London's Victoria Street sitting opposite Dr. Daniel Bartlett, a founder of the Society and a character straight out of a Dickens novel.

Dr. Bartlett was very eager to know my attitude towards the world: did I smoke? did I drink? and – using pronunciation peculiar to himself, did I go to the 'kinema'? As it happened I did none of these things. I have wondered since whether I would have been turned down had I said 'Yes,' to any of these questions.

There were of course questions of deeper significance. I was warned that, in addition to studying for the basic General Ordination Examination, I would also be expected to pass a diploma course on each book of the Bible. I think I gulped a little! It was a daunting prospect for someone who still had to pass his Matriculation. I must have said the right things though because I gained Dr. Bartlett's seal of approval.

It was on a beautiful, clear, October morning that I set out for Bristol with my good friend Albert Croft, who was already a student there, by my side. In my wallet were one hundred pound notes to take care of the cost of my first year's training.

Only that morning I had found at the breakfast table an envelope stuffed with the notes and a lovely letter from my mother. In it she explained that since her marriage she had been a member of the Liverpool Co-operative Society. I knew that only too well because I had often shopped for her and can still remember quoting her number, 30283, with my purchases. The letter said that over the years the dividend had mounted up and never been collected. My mother was purposely saving it up until there came a time when she felt it was really needed. That day, she was sure, had now arrived.

Canon Bernard also informed me that a £100 Bursary would be available to me for a further year's training. A lady from our own parish church had donated funds specifically for the purpose of helping young men from our parish to prepare for the Christian ministry. So it was with a very grateful heart that I set off that October morning.

Saying goodbye to Mum and Dad outside 10, Ogwen Street, was an emotional experience. We had always been a close family. We had had so many wonderful times together and now, as all families have to learn to do, we were splitting up. I should have felt even more choked that morning had I known two things: one was that neither Mum nor Dad was to live long enough to see the fulfilment of their sacrifice . . . the other was that, as I waved goodbye to them, I was also waving goodbye to a working class life.

Theological training, through no fault of those who trained me, was designed not only to equip me for a spiritual ministry in the Anglican Church, but also dramatically to change my lifestyle. In those days particularly a clergyman held a certain status in the community which he could not dismiss. Also he was not expected to be a follower, but a leader . . . a counsellor, advisor, organiser, preacher and friend all in one. He had a secure job, unlike much of the rest of the working class population. He was trusted. He even knew what it was to be in the limelight on occasions.

As far as I recall, none of our neighbours questioned or resented my call to be a clergyman, nor my subsequent change to a middle class lifestyle. It pleased them to know that one of their own was breaking into new territory which was formerly thought of as forbidden territory to working class men. When the day came for my dress and my work to reflect a middle class culture, everybody knew that, at heart, I was still 'one of them'. As indeed I was.

The first person to make an impression on me at college was the Principal, the Rev. W. Dodgson Sykes. He did so on the very first day. There I was, standing idly in my room, feeling out of place, a new boy in every sense of the term, wondering what to do next, when the Principal walked in. He made a habit of welcoming new students individually. It was a commendable practice, but I felt somewhat overawed at meeting the 'great man himself'. I stammered out a few ineffectual words and then the Principal remarked on the coldness of the room. With that he knelt down at the grate and lit the fire. When he was satisfied that it was giving out enough heat to cheer the room he left me. I was to hear the Rev. W. Dodgson Sykes lecture on many occasions during the subsequent three years, but nothing he said could have been more helpful and fitting than that unassuming and humble gesture on the first day.

In fact the Principal was quite a character. He was a keen Puritan, but also a man of great grace. He was very knowledgeable but also very absent-minded! Quite often his lecture notes would rustle to the ground and long minutes passed as he scrambled about on the floor gathering them and we students stifled our mirth as his bald head bobbed up and down behind the lecture rail. And once, at a mealtime, he stood up and bade us be silent for grace. There was a moment's pause. Then he said, 'Clifton 3451' not a new way of addressing the Almighty, but rather the Principal's telephone number!

I suppose there were three lecturers who were to mean most to me at college, men who convinced me of the truth of the Christian Gospel and the validity of the evangelical tradition. They endorsed what I already believed. They helped me to be able to communicate what I knew at heart to be true. One was of course the Principal, another was the Rev. J. Stafford Wright, an outstanding academic and an eminent writer (also an authority on Winnie the Pooh stories which he discussed with almost as much enthusiasm as he discussed theological matters), and the third was a young tutor, Stephen Ensor. He lectured in Greek, but because he also had responsibility for students who were concluding their Matriculation I saw a lot of him. We became close friends and remain so to this day.

Perhaps the greatest joy of that first term was the discovery that the college football team needed a goalkeeper. Football, I discovered, was important. No less a man than the Principal had been heard to remark, 'It has been evident over the years that a good season on the football pitch means a good year in every other sphere of college life'. So Wednesday afternoons found the college team, in our green and black quartered strip, taking on the amateur talent of Bristol. We more than held our own in that company, beating such teams as the Bristol Police Force, Bristol Fire Brigade and Bristol University. But perhaps it gave us keenest pleasure – not a very Christian one! – to beat the local Baptist College! Jim Seddon, I remember, made an excellent captain; Frederick Sprackling was a superb half-back, and two other fine players were John Oliver and Kenneth Coates. I couldn't have performed too badly either. One afternoon the Principal took the trouble to track me down and ask if I could spare an hour or two to coach his twin sons in the art of goalkeeping!

Christmas arrived, and with it the much-looked-forward-to Christmas meal. As always there was a distinguished guest to talk to us and this year it was the elderly and exceedingly deaf Canon Alford. The Principal addressed us first, a little pompously as was his way. 'Take your responsibilities seriously,' he said. 'Just because it's Christmas, don't think of it as a time for slacking. Work hard during the holidays.' Then it was the turn of Canon Alford who, of course, had not heard a word of the Principal's speech. 'Young men,' he declared, 'I have learned throughout my long life that all work and no play makes Jack a dull boy. So go to your homes. Forget your work and come back refreshed for the new term.' Needless to say we had a difficult time restraining our mirth. It was left to our conscience which of the distinguished gentlemen we chose to obey!

My second term was altogether a more eventful one. First I passed Matriculation, which was a great relief and meant I could now concentrate on my theological studies. Secondly I became aware of a marked deterioration in the handwriting in my father's letters. So illegible was it one week that I telephoned a friend in Ogwen Street to make enquiries. He only confirmed my fears. My father had cancer, but neither he nor my mother wanted to interrupt my studies by telling me just how bad it was. I immediately asked for permission to go home for a few days.

I was shattered when I saw my father. It was quite obvious that this dear man, who meant so very much to me domestically, emotionally and spiritually, was fast approaching death. How thankful I have always been that I phoned that friend, for my father died a day or two after my homecoming, on March 25, 1939. In those early days after Dad's death both Mum and I had to discover for ourselves what we had often told others in their bereavement, that death for those in Christ is but a parting for a time; that Christ had promised ultimate victory over death and the grave, and that meantime He was with us, to comfort and strengthen. It was all true of course, but human loss is still a reality and terribly hard to bear. My mother never fully recovered from her husband's death. To an outsider she may have given the impression of being the dominant partner in the marriage, but anyone who really knew them soon realised that this was not the case. She had depended a lot on him.

Later in the year I again saw death at close hand. One bitterly cold November day, during a tough football match, I was injured and, whilst lying on the ground waiting for first aid, I contracted a kidney infection which developed rapidly into pneumonia. I was hurried off to Bristol General Hospital where I spent an uncomfortable few weeks. One day I felt well enough to ignore my own niggling pains and became aware of the man in the next bed, seriously ill and clearly deteriorating every day. Then I heard a doctor tell a nurse that, as the patient had only hours to live, he should be granted any reasonable request. The 'reasonable request' turned out to be a glass of beer, but I was suddenly aware of my own responsibility towards this dying man: beer brought him fleeting enjoyment, Jesus could give him 'a well of water springing up into eternal life.' I prayed for an opportunity to speak to him. Not long after, the man turned to me and I was able to open up a conversation.

I told him about Christ, about my own Christian commitment. I outlined for him the way of salvation and urged him to hand over his life to the Lord. He told me that, for the first time in his life, he really understood what the Gospel was all about. He understood why Christ had come. Hours later, he died – and I believe he went to be with the Saviour.

I recovered slowly and had to take things easily back at college. Studies did not grow any easier, but I was slowly working my way through the books of the Bible for my diploma. Football had to take a back seat for a while, but a less strenuous interest was singing in a college quartet. My three colleagues were Tom Dalby, a fine baritone who was to become a missionary in the Arctic; Robert Mellor, until quite recently a vicar in Tranmere, Birkenhead, and Arthur Goodwin Hudson, an excellent pianist, and a friend of considerable significance in years to come.

Now too was the time when I had my first awakening for the Church overseas. As we prayed in the college chapel for missionaries abroad, as we sang those magnificent missionary hymns from *Hymns of Faith* and the *Keswick Hymnal*, as I heard the names of the

Karamajong in Africa, the wild Naga of Burma and the Eskimo in Baffin Land, I was stirred and fascinated by the limitless vision of world mission. It proved to be a vision I was not going to be able easily to dismiss.

Meanwhile, away from college, studies, missionary hymns and visions, World War Two raged and, as my three years drew to a close, the war took a tight grip on the nation and no end seemed in sight. As theological students we were given the choice by the Government: we could suspend our studies and join the Forces with the Government's promise that we could conclude our studies when the war ended, or, if our diocese consented, we could be ordained and serve the Church at home. As I was in debt to the Liverpool diocese for my third year's training, I travelled home to consult the diocesan authorities. The Bishop did not hesitate; he needed more ordained men to help at such a critical time.

Liverpool was suffering under fierce air raids. As I wandered the streets by day I saw only utter devastation. Landmarks I had grown up with and cherished were smashed down, streets were packed high with rubble, people shuffled by, their eyes dulled with fatigue, sadness and fear. Olive was working in a children's hospital which one night was hit directly by a bomb. Miraculously the bomb exploded outwards rather than inwards thus sparing many lives. Olive's hearing, already slightly impaired, was damaged for life however.

Olive escaped, my mother did not. One night, in May 1941, during a terrifying air raid in which 2,000 people lost their lives, she suffered a mild stroke. I was with her and called for an ambulance. It arrived eventually, already packed with casualties from the streets. There was no room for me.

As the ambulance moved off I searched out my old faithful Rudge Whitworth bicycle, scarred with rust, battered by time, but still – thank God – usable. I shall never forget that ride through the streets of Liverpool; the city was literally burning down around me. I was stopped about a dozen times by air raid wardens who shouted at me to take cover, but I was determined to keep the ambulance in sight. That was not too difficult: the streets were littered with blazing debris and the ambulance was reduced to running let alone cycling pace. At one point all traffic was halted by a blazing bus which threatened to blow up. The ambulance was allowed through and I sneaked through after it, unnoticed.

Finally the ambulance and the Rudge Whitworth arrived simultaneously outside the hospital. I don't think the ambulance driver could believe his eyes when he jumped out of his cab and spotted me astride my bike. My mother showed no surprise though. She knew I would make it somehow!

I was at my mother's side for two days and then she quietly and peacefully died. I was so thankful that I had been with her when she most needed me, just as in happier days she had always been there when I needed her.

I had enjoyed a blessed and happy childhood, enriched by dear and wonderful parents. But now I had to face the fact that it was all over. My parents were dead. I was an adult. Adjustments had to be made. A new life beckoned to me, but I did not have to face it alone; I had Olive.

6: Wartime Curate

The Principal spotted me as I entered the room to take my final General Ordination exams and remarked, 'Oh my dear Sutton! You don't stand a dog's chance. But do your best!' It was May, 1941. Few parts of the country were escaping the fierce enemy air attacks and Bristol was no exception. There were several air raid alerts during the course of the exams and one major disturbance when a huge bomb dropped nearby on the downs. We had to make a note in the margin of our paper every time such a disruption occurred and for how long. I am convinced that very generous allowances were made for this, because I passed.

I left college with mixed feelings. My days there had been an enriching experience. With hindsight, I realise that the actual study for the General Ordination Exam had little relevance to the practical work of the ministry. But just being with the diversity of people among the students and lecturers, taught me much. I also felt sure that my own deep personal experiences during the three years would stand me in good stead. Perhaps above all I had enjoyed the intimate study of the Bible.

My convictions as a conservative evangelical were not formed at college, nor from reading or through the influence of any one person. I am a Protestant by instinct. It was an inner conviction I had even as a young man before I was converted. At college the teaching and writings of W. Dodgson Sykes and J. Stafford Wright endorsed all I already believed. They underlined and helped me to verbalise truths that were already vital to me.

I therefore left college with an even clearer conviction of the complete authority and inspiration of the Bible. I also firmly believed in the priesthood of all believers. I could not then, and cannot still, reconcile an elitism in the ministry with the Scriptures. Above all, I believed passionately that all need to be saved through faith in the Lord Jesus Christ. He *alone* is the Saviour of the world. I cherished a deep desire to see the world won for Christ, so evangelism was most important to me.

Shortly before ordination, I joined the five day retreat for ordinands at St. Deiniol's Library at Hawarden in Wales. This residential library houses the 30,000 books belonging to the great Prime Minister, William Gladstone, a devout high churchman. The house looked out over the Dee Estuary and the Wirral. In the distance, on a clear day, Liverpool, to which I was soon to return for my first curacy, could be seen. The Warden who led the retreat was the Reverend Doctor Alec Vidler, a renowned scholar, author, theologian and priest. He was very liberal in his attitude to the Christian faith and called himself an 'agnostic believer'.

Towards the end of the retreat I was interviewed by Dr. David, the Bishop of Liverpool. He was a wise, gracious man whose advice I respected. He urged me, as a declared conservative evangelical Christian, not to allow my very clear convictions to make me arrogant. He encouraged me to keep my mind open to those whose beliefs contradicted my own. By being prepared to listen, I could enrich my mind and my life. He stated very clearly his observation that people with very definite theological views – *of whatever shade* – so often lacked grace and tolerance. It was advice I have needed to recall over the years!

The only cloud over my bright, sunny ordination day

was that my parents were not there to share it. Although, in spirit, I could sense their presence. Olive and my brothers and their families were at the service. The Bishop's address laid great emphasis on the fact that a new era had dawned in the Church of England. Of the 25 men to be ordained that day, for the first time 15 were from a working class background. A little piece of history was being made!

I was not broken gently into my first curacy. I had been appointed to serve in the parish of Emmanuel Church, Fazakerley, near Aintree Racecourse, under the Vicar, Albert Simmonds. It was a very large parish with 30,000 people and there were also two daughter churches: St. Paul's and St. George's. I was the junior member of the team which included two other curates, John Barrow and Douglas Hesketh, and a Church Army Captain, Bertie Harris.

After my ordination service I just had time for lunch with Olive before I reported for duty and found myself, quite unexpectedly, addressing the Sunday afternoon Bible Class. The vicar took me along and introduced me and I was ready to take my seat alongside the rest. But no – he said he had a lot of other things to attend to, so he would leave it to me. It was, I suppose, a good test of initiative!

I was ready with my sermon for Evening Prayer. I preached on the verse which meant a great deal to me: 'Therefore being justified by faith, we have peace with God through our Lord Jesus Christ.' (Romans 1. 15).

That was not the end of my day's work. As the leader of the youth fellowship failed to turn up after the evening service, I was pushed in there too. I really needed my sleep that night! But it was not long before I discovered that this was fairly typical of life at Emmanuel.

My digs at 11, Garden Lane, were a little touch of heaven on earth. I rented a room in the home of a

Christian couple of rare calibre, Doris and Alfred Hunter. Doris Hunter was, at one time, a missionary in China and her husband was an engineer. They had two teenage sons, Leo and John Gaunt Hunter, and it was an added pleasure to join in their family life. I was thrilled to be able to share my experience of Christ with the boys and to see them come to the Lord during the time I was in Fazakerley. Both boys were later ordained and our lives were to have other fascinating points of contact in the coming years.

Olive was always made welcome too in the Hunters' home. She had been working in a Liverpool Children's Hospital while I was at college. When I was appointed to Fazakerley, she obtained a post in a private home in Maghull, four or five miles away. She was keen to be near me and to be able to share in the work as much as possible. The father of the children whom she minded was fulfilling a confidential role 'strategic to the war effort'.

Emmanuel, Fazakerley, was a CPAS parish though a little broader in its churchmanship than I was used to. I found myself the most conservative evangelical member of the staff, but we worked well together. It was a lively church with large congregations. The war was still raging and there was a large RAF camp close by so, in order to cater for the large numbers and the diversity of visitors from the camp, the Vicar found it necessary to have two services of Evening Prayer. He was a man who enjoyed innovation. The 6 p.m. service followed the traditional Prayer Book, whereas the 7.15 service was quite informal.

With busy Sundays at the three churches and a full midweek programme, there was not a lot of time to spare. If, after that first Sunday, I had not realised how versatile the junior curate was expected to be, the fact certainly came home a week later. On the Monday morning I was presented with a tin of whitewash and a large brush and instructed to paint the walls of the old church hall toilets. I was not too happy about it, feeling that I had not been ordained for such a task. But of course these were hard times with the war consuming so much manpower.

I gratefully received my wages of £260 a year and was gradually managing to pay back the £100 loaned by the diocese. My chief incentive was that I could only marry Olive when the debt was fully paid. It was not always easy for Olive to make the four to five mile journey on her bicycle to be with us for worship and midweek meetings, but she was not one to make excuses or to be easily deterred. It was after a particularly fierce snow storm in the early months of 1942 that my Vicar found out why I was not yet in a position to marry. One by one, young people were arriving in the church vestry for the youth group's annual general meeting. Only a few had turned up as the snow was at least a foot deep and continuing to drive down. As we peered out of the window trying to identify the young people as they emerged out of the gloom, the Vicar remarked that this was one meeting Olive certainly would not manage to attend. Almost as he spoke, what looked like a moving snowman could be seen staggering up Longmore Lane dragging a totally useless bicycle behind it. Yes, it was Olive – very bedraggled indeed but determined, as ever, to be there.

My Vicar had been noticing increasingly that, by having me on his staff, he had an extra member in Olive and he asked me why we did not make life more simple for ourselves by getting married. I explained the situation and, as Albert Simmonds was never a man to let the grass grow under his feet, he went the very next day to consult with a member of the Diocesan Finance Board. He returned, delighted to inform me that I could marry Olive whenever we were ready and that the repayment of the relatively small proportion of the loan had been waived. I never found out, but always suspected that the Vicar himself paid it off.

The wedding was a truly family affair although neither of us had parents to share in the wonderful day. All those who have any recollections of any cause to celebrate during the war years, will have similar stories to tell of great initiative, innovation and unselfishness as precious food coupons were shared and swapped and saved in order to accumulate sufficient food worthy of a celebration. People were generous with their clothing coupons and helped Olive to buy material for her dress and those of the bridesmaids. One of the churchwardens was a grocer and he put aside little extras for us month by month.

All the excited preparations culminated in a glorious day of rejoicing on September 6, 1942. It poured with rain but we hardly noticed. Best Man was my old college friend John Oliver, and Olive chose two of her best friends as bridesmaids. The whole church came to the wedding and joined in the celebrations afterwards. And, as at the wedding in Cana of Galilee, Jesus was at the centre of all our joy.

Towards evening, Olive and I left the church, still celebrating, to make our way to Fleetwood from which port the Steam Packet Boat Company ran a service to Douglas on the Isle of Man. We stayed in Glen Auldyn for a wonderful week's honeymoon in the mellow Autumn sunshine. Then we returned home ready for what we had been anticipating for four years: the opportunity to serve the Lord *together*. We spent the first few weeks of our married life still in the Hunters' home, but soon a furnished house in Longmore Lane became available to us to rent and we moved into the larger premises.

Christmasses had always been special to me and our first married Christmas was no exception. Olive saved up the food coupons and, after a morning of church services, we sat down to enjoy the most minute shoulder of lamb one could possibly imagine. But it tasted wonderful and we were so glad to be together. After lunch, we were to forge one of the friendships that has meant so much to us over the years. We were invited to the home of our church organist, Fred Nicholson and his wife. Fred was then in his late sixties – an architect, no mean artist, and a fine musician. His delightful wife was very old fashioned indeed, an earnest Christian lady who saw some spiritual significance in the most mundane details of life. Their daughter, Winifred, had recently married my predecessor at Emmanuel Church, John Arthur Briggs, who was now a curate at Norris Green. Winifred and Arthur, Olive and I immediately 'clicked'. We became firm friends and found we had much in common. Arthur and I particularly shared an intense amusement in some of old Mrs. Nicholson's quaint, spiritual observations. We sometimes found it very difficult not to disgrace ourselves, to the great embarrassment of our wives, by dissolving into laughter at some of her unlikely pronouncements. But we loved and respected her deeply nonetheless.

A sense of fun was not a bad trait to take with me into my next challenge as a curate. John Barrow, our senior curate, moved on and I was put in charge of St. George's, the daughter church which served the Sparrow Hall housing estate. A great majority of Sparrow Hall was inhabited by those who had been rehoused from the slums of Liverpool. Many had not adapted happily to being uprooted and were finding it hard socially to adjust.

During the 1930s, small daughter churches like St.George's had sprung up all over Liverpool to cater for those large housing estates being erected to relieve slum areas. I was dubious about the concept of daughter churches right from the start and I think my misgivings have been proved valid by the experience of the years.

The problems are twofold and neither has been successfully overcome. A daughter church is reliant for its upkeep to a great extent on the parish church. Therefore it is *not* autonomous and resents the fact that final decisions are made on its behalf at parish church level. Additionally, the daughter church is usually put in the care of a curate in charge who, no sooner does he endear himself to his people and identify with the area, when he has to move on and thereby destroy any continuity in the ministry.

St. George's, Fazakerley, also had the disadvantage of being a dual purpose building. It was virtually impossible, therefore, simply by drawing aside a screen on a Sunday, to eradicate the secular atmosphere created by whist drives, dances, billiards and darts from Monday to Saturday. The very first weekend I was in charge of the church, late on the Saturday evening, I had to negotiate a rough and rowdy group of people outside the church which was really the only open space available to them.

After two years in Fazakerley, my vicar moved on to a parish in Halifax. I was sad to see him go because I had learned so much from him and admired him greatly. Nevertheless his successor, John William Hartshorn, was an outstanding evangelical clergyman holding in fact convictions much nearer my own than had Albert Simmonds. I was permitted to remain at St. George's for a while until the new vicar settled in.

But a few months later we were on the move. My great friend, Jim Seddon, was serving a curacy at St. Philemon, Toxteth Park, but he and Mavis, his wife, had been called by God to serve overseas. They had applied to the BCMS and were accepted for service in Morocco. St. Philemon's required a curate with some experience because the vicar, Canon Thomas Copner, was over 80 years old and only took services three times a year – at Easter, Harvest and Christmas. The curate was thus virtually in charge. So it was that the Bishop asked John Hartshorn if he would release me and allow me to serve at St. Philemon's.

It was a wrench to leave the parish which held such precious and significant memories of our marriage and first curacy. But we were prepared and went to settle into our new parish. We were given a rough inauguration when a murder was committed on our very first night there, only a few doors along the road. St. Philemon's was an inner city parish near the Dock Road and the pressures of war intensified what was already a tough social situation.

My first weekend at St. Philemon's holds an outstanding memory. I rushed back on the Saturday afternoon from seeing Jim and Mavis Seddon off at Lime Street Station, to take two weddings. One of Jim's last jobs had been to fill in the details in the marriage register for me. I was not to know that the forms concerning the 3 p.m. wedding had been left on top of those for the 2 p.m. service. So I went ahead and proceeded to marry – say – Mary Smith to Bill Jones. As far as I could tell the couple readily replied 'I will' when I invited Bill to take Mary and Mary to take Bill as respective partners. Imagine my utter astonishment when the time came for the registers to be signed! It was only then that I realised the mistake I had made – I had used the names for the 3 p.m. service to follow!

In utter bewilderment I asked the bride and groom why ever they had answered to the wrong names. They replied that they had assumed they were set piece names used for every wedding. An updated version of the N or M of the Catechism I suppose! Incredible but true! On the spur of the moment I wondered what I should do and decided to go through the relevant part of the service again in the vestry using the right names – which turned out to be legally acceptable. Ever since, I have been extra cautious in checking my facts before a wedding!

During my time in Toxteth I served as an ARP warden. The devastation and carnage appalled me. The contrast between these scenes and the loving, caring atmosphere I had known and thrived on as a boy in Ogwen Street, was totally incomprehensible. Man's inhumanity to man would be a cause of utter hopelessness and mystery if it were not for the biblical doctrine of sin and God's plan of salvation. Sin has the power to destroy an individual life and in war time that destruction is poured out on a massive scale.

One small incident in my experience as an ARP warden summed up the utter futility of war. As I dragged out the body of an old lady from beneath the rubble of her little terraced house, I thought of the joy and comfort she had no doubt brought to her family and neighbours over the years. It was all snuffed out under a pile of rubble. There were very deep political issues behind the war, but these all seemed far away and irrelevant in the light of individual human suffering. All around me there lived children deprived of fathers and young wives separated from their husbands.

I was and remain convinced that the only force worth pursuing is love. Love has proved effective in my own life on many occasions and one can only rejoice in the increasing number of illustrations around the world today which demonstrate that power. There are innumerable instances of Christian love selflessly given every day, but they never make the headlines.

My new vicar, Canon Copner, was virtually the last in a line of Puritan, evangelical clergymen who had known personally the first great Bishop of Liverpool, John Charles Ryle. He rarely went out but, if he did, he was readily distinguished by his long walrus moustache and flat pancake cap. So venerated a figure was he that the ladies still spontaneously curtseyed to him in the street! His study was a sight to behold. The walls were systematically lined with row upon row of brown paper bags. Inside each bag was a sermon written in pefect copper-plate handwriting. Canon Copner continued to write sermons for each Sunday of the year although most of them were never delivered. Under his leadership over many years, however, St. Philemon's had become a stronghold of evangelicalism and at the heart of its congregation was a large core of committed and active Christians.

One of my duties was to serve as an honorary Chaplain to the 5th Regiment of the Maritime Artillery stationed in the barracks in Windsor Street. For two years I made it my job to visit the barracks almost every day if possible. I was able to do a little social work there as well as conduct services. There were a few conversions among the men and their families and it was a great joy, for many years afterwards, to hear from these Christians stationed in various parts of the world witnessing for the Lord.

A few months after my arrival the vicar died. He had always been a strong patriot and supporter of the Church Lads' Brigade and his funeral reflected both facts: his coffin was draped with a Union Jack and the Brigades' buglers sounded the last post and reveille at the graveside. It was the end of an era.

It was the end of an era for me too. The events that followed were sad and uncharacteristic of my experience in the ministry until then. Dr. David's successor as Bishop of Liverpool, Dr. Clifford Martin, asked me to remain at St. Philemon's until a new vicar was appointed to succeed Canon Copner. I willingly consented and continued with the work as before. Soon afterwards however, while Olive and I were out of the parish for a few days' break, the Parochial Church Council, quite without my knowledge, wrote to the Bishop asking if I could become Canon Copner's permanent successor. The Bishop naturally assumed that I had instigated this request and was very angry. I was very sad because it meant leaving my ministry in Liverpool on a sour note.

A new vicar was eventually appointed and I was invited to become a curate to my former vicar, Canon Arthur Gore Bernard. He was no longer at my old Emmanuel Church, but had moved to a very upper middle class parish on the Wirral Peninsula. Bebington Parish Church was an ancient building which had once been a hospice for ailing monks from Chester. Canon Bernard was having some problems because his predecessor had been a conservative evangelical, as were most of the congregation. Canon Bernard, although a low churchman, was not evangelistic in his outlook. I looked upon my new role as something of a go-between: I knew Canon Bernard well, but I was also fully in sympathy with the views of his congregation.

Sadly, Canon Bernard had a tendency in Bebington to upset all sorts of people. One memorable December day he chose to upset all the Funeral Directors in the district so that they all refused to dig graves for him as part of their work. In fact it was the church's responsibility to perform this task and the undertakers only usually did so as a favour to most vicars, and were paid accordingly. Crisis point arrived because the funeral of a very important personage was due the next day and the undertakers flatly refused to go beyond their bounds of duty. The vicar arrived flustered and angry at our little house in St. Andrew's Drive and instructed me that there was no alternative, I would have to prepare the grave for the imminent funeral.

There was no way I was going to do the digging in broad daylight, so Olive and I waited until dark. We set off with a storm lantern and large spade. The scene in the graveyard would have done justice to any Bronte novel: it poured with rain and the wind howled. Olive stood trying to hold the lantern still while I dug for all I was worth. Everything went wrong. I encountered obstructions, the sides kept caving in, and the hole kept filling with water. I later learned that a stream ran beneath the churchyard! After a long struggle, however, the job was reasonably complete. I shored up the sides and fervently hoped the trench would still be there in the morning. Thankfully it was, and I imagine Canon Bernard made peace with the undertakers because it was the only time I was called upon to perform the task of a gravedigger.

As in my first curacy at Fazakerley, it was the young people's work at Bebington which was a source of particular joy and encouragement. We had around us a fine group of Christian young people, several of whom were to enter full time Christian service. We have remained specially close over the years to Norah Howlett who married the Rev. Kenneth White and went to serve the Lord in Africa before coming home to a fine ministry in England. Ken is at present vicar of Totland near Freshwater on the Isle of Wight and we value their friendship deeply.

We were not at Bebington for a full two years but one of the most outstanding events in any young couple's life occurred during that time. A month late and across the Mersey in a Liverpool nursing home, our daughter Janet was born. When I saw her for the first time, in my typical emotional way, I wept: but they were tears of joy. We were thrilled. Looking back, as Janet has proved such a magnificent daughter, our joy and gratitude at her birth have been well justified.

But the time of my curacies was drawing to a close. As I reflect on these years of 'apprenticeship', I can still only say how abundantly blessed we were by God as we sought to serve Him in the three very different areas of Fazakerley, Toxteth and Bebington. I was not the most prepared of men for the ministry, but God was wonderfully faithful.

7: Beside the Seaside

After five years as a curate in three contrasting Merseyside parishes, an unexpected letter changed the direction of my life. It came from a friend, the Reverend Maurice Jones, Vicar of St. Mary, Kirkdale and a trustee of Christ Church, Lowestoft, Suffolk. He wanted to put forward my name for the vacant living there. As always, Olive and I were content to commit the possibility to the Lord.

A few weeks later I was invited to view the parish and, with mixed feelings, I crossed the country by rail. The parish is the most easterly in the British Isles, situated on Ness Point. I was met at the station by two senior members of the church, George Pretty, the local coal merchant, and Arthur Moore, a grocer. I soon realised that they were men of great spiritual maturity: old fashioned evangelical Christians who believed firmly in the inspiration and authority of the Bible. I warmed to them immediately.

Signs that Lowestoft had been a Royal Navy Depot during the war were still evident in 1946. The Church was windowless and the parish hall remained in the hands of the Navy. All around was dereliction and, to add to the problems, the vicarage was due for imminent demolition in a road widening scheme. As I walked and talked that day, I sensed a great need both materially and spiritually in this devastated area. To round off the visit, I was invited to share in a church prayer meeting in Swiss Cottage, the home of Mr. Salter and his wife. There were about twelve fairly elderly members present as most of the younger folk were still attached to the armed forces. If I had any doubts as to whether or not I should accept this parish, they were totally dispelled during that prayer time. Heaven came down: it was one of the finest prayer meetings I have ever attended. These, I sensed, were wonderful Christian people, among whom it would be a glorious privilege to serve.

I shared my conviction with Olive and in due course I was appointed Vicar of Christ Church. Although we looked forward with joyful anticipation to our new ministry, we left Bebington with heavy hearts. We had such happy memories of our curacy days, of friendships forged and of Janet's arrival. But that era in our lives was now over. So too, happily, was the war, and it was a time of new beginnings for all.

In the absence of a vicarage, a flat had been found for us to live in, about a mile from the church. But it was not quite ready for occupation for the first few days and we stayed in a small local hotel. On our first evening in Lowestoft, we went for a walk and slipped into a fish and chip shop. The gentleman behind the counter asked where we came from. We chatted and I told him I had been appointed the new vicar of Christ Church. He warmly welcomed us and introduced himself as Ned Goldspink: he and his family were keen members of Christ Church and they had been looking forward to having us with them. Little did we know on that September evening that their son, Robert, was one day to become one of my finest curates!

Another wonderful friendship was forged in the earliest days, originally through rather adverse circumstances. Our baby daughter was a toddler by now and had managed to tumble down the stairs and break a leg. On hearing of the accident, one of those who came to offer condolences was the rector of a neighbouring parish, the Reverend Stanley Pert of St. Michael's, Oulton. As the months went by, we were to realise that we had much in common with Stanley and Retta Pert and another cherished lifetime's friendship became firmly rooted. It was at the rectory of St. Michael's that we spent our Christmasses during our Lowestoft days.

Gradually as 1946 gave way to 1947, the young people were being demobilised and returning home. The Navy eventually vacated the parish hall and the government granted us compensation for war damage so that windows were restored and other essential repairs carried out. It had taken us no time to realise that we had around us a group of wonderfully mature Christian people and now, with the added youthful manpower, we were ready for action. After months in makeshift accommodation, a lovely vicarage was purchased in Station Road and we gratefully moved in. The summer of 1947 saw us on the march.

As a seaside resort which drew holidaymakers in the summer, our open air ministry was a speciality. We had a lay reader, Daniel Stern, who was especially gifted in this type of work. True to his name, he was a real Daniel: a man of unshakeable convictions who fearlessly and faithfully proclaimed the Gospel. Every Tuesday evening throughout the summer, we would go out and about fishing for men in the open air. Daniel's open air sermons were full of fire and judgement and I trembled with fear every time he spoke. It was not the message that worried me, but the fact that his false teeth worked loose as he preached and I could see him choking!

The spring of 1948 was special to us in a very personal way because God blessed us with a baby son. John was born in Lowestoft Hospital in April that year and our hearts were in our mouths as we allowed little Janet to carry her baby brother proudly out of the hospital to a waiting car!

On Sunday nights we invited some notable preachers of the day to Christ Church. I.E. Davidson of the Barbican Mission to the Jews and Jack Dain of the Bible Medical and Missionary Fellowship were just two of the outstanding preachers. We were also enriched by the ministry of missionaries home on furlough, particularly that of Alan Neech, our link missionary in India, who was much later to become the General Secretary of BCMS.

In this way the summer was packed with evangelistic activity both within and outside the church. It was an exciting ministry with very many conversions. It was always important of course that our own church people should be well fed and nourished spiritually and at first an important help was our link with Christian Endeavour, an interdenominational fellowship of believers. There was great emphasis on prayer and Bible study within Christian Endeavour and one most important aspect was that it encouraged lay people to participate in leadership. The vicar's night occurred just once a month: each week otherwise it was a lay member of the congregation who led our devotions and study. Week after week our dingy choir vestry would come alive with spiritual vitality as we met to glorify Christ and to learn more about Him. As time progressed, our own church Bible study and prayer meeting took over pre-eminence as our weekly gathering. These soon flourished and, if there was any dissent at all at our midweek meetings, it was when we discussed the Second Coming of Christ. We were all agreed that He *will* come again, but there were those, like so many through the ages, who chose to ignore Jesus's warning that the timing of this climax of history is quite outside human calculation. They had fixed ideas as to when Jesus would return and eloquently tried to convince us all that they were right.

In the late summer, as the surge of visiting

holidaymakers began to recede, a new influx of visitors arrived. These were literally hundreds of Scottish fisherfolk who travelled south with the herring and mackerel each year. They stopped at ports along the coast from the north east of Scotland southwards and Lowestoft was their most southerly and final port of call. Each day the men would go out to fish, and their wives, on shore, would be ready to receive the catch, gut clean and salt the fish ready for sale at home and abroad. Although staunch, fundamental Nonconformists, many of the fisherfolk joined us on a Sunday and their Scottish fishermen's choirs enriched our worship. They sang in beautiful harmony, mainly the old fashioned Moody and Sankey hymns.

At the close of the fishing season, as winter was creeping on, the church was packed to overflowing for the Harvest of the Sea Festival. This was a true Harvest Thanksgiving when the regular congregation joined with the fishermen and their families to thank God for a harvest of fish safely gathered in from the murky waters of the North Sea. The church was suitably decorated with fishing nets and buoys and lanterns. Uncannily, within a few hours the next day, these hundreds of Scottish visitors vanished from the beaches, streets and fields of Lowestoft, returning home like migrant swallows. We knew they would all be back next September.

In addition to our efforts as a church to take the Gospel to the people of Lowestoft and to holidaymakers, we also organised several lively evangelistic campaigns. My deeply respected friends from the NYLC, Frederick and Arthur Wood, led one very fruitful campaign, and another, which met with much positive response, was led by Tom Rees. By way of follow up, I instigated, with Stanley Pert's full support and backed by a team of loyal committed helpers, what we called 'Christian Rendezvous' in the town. The aim was to strengthen young Christians in their faith and to equip them better for Christian witness and service. We organised a monthly meeting in the Methodist Church to start with. But we soon outgrew those premises and moved to the Central Baptist Church which held a key position in the town with good parking facilities. Several hundred people attended each month and we invited well known Christian speakers of the day to address them, among them Hugh Redwood, Gladys Aylward, the Wood brothers and Tom Rees.

One result of this was to unite the churches in the area, most of which supported Christian Rendezvous. Just how united we were was seen when the issue of Sunday cinema came very much to the fore. Today, of course, there is still a hot debate on the issue of Sunday trading; equally hot then was the issue of Sunday cinema. Each municipality was instructed to ballot its constituents in order to find out the wishes of the people locally. As Christians we were opposed to this and were not afraid to say so. The cinema management were, on the other hand, just as keen to have the opportunity to open up and make more business for themselves. A referendum was called in Lowestoft and the two camps busily organised campaigns to win people to their point of view. The Mayor ruefully told me that there was much more enthusiasm being shown over this one issue than there ever was for the regular elections to the Town Council!

On the day itself, the cinema organised a grand parade of floats with open tableaux urging people to vote for their cause. One float had a caricature picture of myself and a large banner on which was inscribed in bold letters, 'DON'T TAKE ANY NOTICE OF THE JEREMIAH. VOTE IN FAVOUR OF SUNDAY CINEMA!' Not to be outdone, some supporters of Christian Rendezvous quickly concocted a float of their own with the wording, 'JEREMIAH WAS THE ONLY RIGHTEOUS MAN IN AN UNRIGHTEOUS GENERATION!' The two opposing campaigns were good humoured, but very much in earnest!

Finally the churches narrowly lost the vote and the way opened up for the cinemas to do business on the Sabbath. Nevertheless the ensuing months were ones in which the churches in Lowestoft grew significantly both numerically and spiritually. God blessed us in a wonderful way, drawing many people to Himself. Christ Church was full Sunday by Sunday and Stanley Pert in the neighbouring parish was experiencing outstanding blessing too.

As I entered my fifth year at Lowestoft, letters began to arrive from the Church Pastoral Aid Society inviting me to consider moving to parishes of which they were trustees. We refused all such invitations until St. Mark's Church, Layton, Blackpool, came to our attention. God made it very clear that we should not just turn this down, so Olive and I spent a day looking the church over.

The church building itself was of outstanding beauty. We discovered that the previous vicar, William Evans, had ministered in the church for thirty years, right up to the Sunday before his death through cancer. He was a greatly loved man who, I was told, would be impossible to replace. His comparatively young widow and two children were to remain in the parish living, in fact, in the house they had always occupied which belonged to them. So there was no vicarage. The traditional churchmanship of St. Mark's was low but by no means evangelical and the parishioners wished it to remain that way. Additionally the church was heavily in debt.

But the Lord insisted that this *was* the place for us. I had met with St. Mark's two churchwardens, William Doxey and Lillian Chew, and despite all the apparently adverse circumstances, they guaranteed me their unconditional support if I agreed to go to St. Mark's. As we looked around the parish that day, I spotted a row of houses near the church and asked whether there might be any possibility of renting one of them. We were told that was highly unlikely.

So God seemed to set His seal on our decision to move to Blackpool when, quite unexpectedly and miraculously, a house in the very row of houses I had spotted, became vacant to rent. In fact, in the few days after we had moved in and before I was instituted as vicar, I had the great joy of leading a girl to the Lord in our new house, which seemed to be a further seal of God's approval.

Our leaving Lowestoft was a highly emotional occasion. I was leaving behind so many dearly loved and respected co-workers in the Gospel. To make matters worse, there were several level crossings on the railway line out of Lowestoft and, at each of these, a sizeable crowd had gathered to wave us on our way. I unashamedly wept and Olive had to explain to other passengers the cause of my distress. I believe they found it quite moving that a parson could become so involved with his people that he was reduced to such a state!

I was instituted as vicar of St. Mark's, Layton, in January 1951. We were very conscious indeed of all the problems in our path, but we were equally aware that we would not be coping with them alone. We were confident that we were in the place of God's choice.

One way in which God blessed us very early on was in the establishment of a very happy relationship with the previous vicar's widow. Mary Evans was much younger than her husband and had been left with two comparatively young children. We sensed an immediate affinity with Mary and were able to help her to arrange for her children to attend two very good boarding schools. Much later we were to learn that our happy relationship with Mary had softened the attitude of many in the parish who had been determined not to co operate with the successor to her husband whom they had admired so much.

Sunday evening congregations had dwindled, although there was an excellent 40 strong choir. Midweek activities abounded and flourished. Apart from all possible uniformed organisations, there were two dramatic societies, a regular whist drive and dance. It was contrary to all my convictions that a church's strength should lie in all these secular pursuits. Thus, at an early meeting of the Parochial Church Council, I ventured to suggest that I would like to replace the Tuesday evening whist drive with a weekly Bible study and prayer meeting. One of the members retorted, 'Well, I 'ope it keeps fine for thee, vicar. Who d'yer thinks goin' to turn out to a Bible Study and prayer meeting every week?' I quietly pointed out that at least God would be there, Olive would be there and I would be there. Lillian Chew and Will Doxey, the churchwardens, true to their word, also voiced their support. In fact, as the weeks went by, God blessed the midweek meeting and numbers grew dramatically. Soon all secular activities receded as the spiritual life of the church flourished.

Another matter over which members of the PCC took issue with me early on, was that of how to settle the huge debt. This had been incurred through the building of a new hall for which there had been inadequate money supply. One of my first jobs at St. Mark's was to arrange for the official opening of the hall, to be named the William Evans Memorial Hall, in memory of the previous vicar. Then came the problem of paying for it.

I expressed my belief that, as we consecrated the hall to God for His use, He would provide the money to pay off the debt. Most members of the PCC felt that the safest way was to rely on raffles, whist drives and other social functions. However, a small group of us began to pray that the Lord would provide through direct giving and the money began slowly to trickle in. One day I was walking along Westcliff Drive when an old lady with a white stick approached from the opposite direction. I stopped and introduced myself as the new vicar of St. Mark's. 'I was on my way to see you!' the old lady said. 'I want you to know that I have heard about you and I am totally in agreement with your principles. I was coming to bring you a present.'

She pushed a brown paper parcel tied with string into my hand, for which I thanked her and we parted. It was some time later in the day that I bothered to open the parcel which I thought probably contained some old books. But imagine my astonishment when out tumbled over a thousand pound notes! The PCC could not believe it when I reported how incredibly our prayer had been answered.

But there was more to come. The blind old lady died soon afterwards and, in her will, left half her money to the church and half to a charity. We thought this would probably not amount to a great deal as she lived very humbly in a tiny terraced house. But inside was discovered a chest of drawers crammed full with more pound notes. Thanks to that little old lady, our immediate financial problems were well and truly solved. And God had honoured, in the most unexpected way, our trust in Him.

Not long after my arrival at St. Mark's I had another surprise of a different nature. I was preparing the church for the evening service one Sunday when a large van pulled up outside. Three young men entered and calmly told me that they had come for the chairs. (Our church had beautiful oak chairs instead of pews.) I must have looked shocked because they quickly explained that they were from the Working Men's Club and it was customary for them to borrow the chairs whenever they needed them. I found my voice and protested that we were holding a service of worship any minute and the chairs would be needed for that. But surely, they argued, very few chairs would be needed for the service. In fact, the evening congregations had been large since my arrival: many people were still coming out of curiosity to see the new vicar! But I told them, in faith, that the day of their borrowing the chairs was over: they would always be needed in church from now on.

It was a year before a real breakthrough in numbers occurred. In February 1952, along with all the other Anglican churches in the land, we held a memorial service for the late King George VI. The church was packed out for that service and continued to be full every Sunday evening from then on. During the time of the Blackpool illuminations we even had to put up 'Church Full' notices and direct visitors to other churches in the town. One year the press took a photograph of the very long queue of people waiting to enter church for the 8 a.m. Holy Communion Service as those attending at 7 a.m. were still inside. The caption asked, 'Guess what these people are queuing for?' and it made a few suggestions. Then it surprised its readers with the news that they were actually queuing to go to church.

God provided some fine helpers in the ministry at Blackpool. Robert Goldspink, whom we knew so well from Lowestoft days, was my curate for four years and he and his wife Kathleen were a superb team. Their contibution to the life and work at St. Mark's cannot be overestimated. Albert Brown, later to become Archdeacon of Ruanda, and his wife Jean, joined us. Albert was a fine Bible expositor and I readily put him in charge of the midweek Bible study. Jack Wardle also became one of my curates and brought a new dimension of friendship and pastoral care to the work. Together with his wife, Jean, he had a special concern for young people. We were also honoured to have as a curate the

Rev. Theo Benson, a fine man of God who was recuperating from an illness contracted while a missionary in China. There was also a Church Army Sister, Kathy McEvoy, who could preach as well as the best of us and was another invaluable member of the team.

While curates came and went however, constantly by my side was Olive. She took responsibility for the women's work at St. Mark's, introducing the CPAS Women's Action as well as supporting the fast growing Mothers' Union. Even now, thirty years on, Olive keeps in touch with some of the ladies in those groups at Blackpool, so strong was their bond of friendship.

Olive, with Robert Goldspink, was also responsible for establishing a Sunday School which grew in the most remarkable way. There was a large housing estate on our doorstep, the Grange Park Estate. It was situated in the neighbouring parish of Poulton, but was a long way from Poulton Church. The vicar readily permitted us to open a Sunday School on the estate. It had modest beginnings: in the home of a friend. But it expanded rapidly so that Olive and Robert, with a growing team of leaders, moved into the day school premises in order to accommodate all the children. Many youngsters were converted at the Grange Park Sunday School.

Our own two children were growing up fast. By now, Janet had gained a place at the Arnold High School for girls. John was an enthusiastic footballer in true Sutton tradition and he attended the local Layton Primary School. One of the highlights of my week was to support the school football team when they played matches on Saturday mornings. Our team won the Blackpool Schools Championship for two seasons when John was involved. The football may not have been quite up to the standard of those matches thirty years before at the Kop, but the atmosphere was charged with the same excitement and enthusiasm!

For one season however my Saturday mornings were

absorbed elsewhere. One of my regular congregation, Alderman Harold Grimbledeston, was elected Mayor. He asked me to be his chaplain. Olive and I accompanied Norah and Harold Grimbledeston on many of their official functions that year and regularly, on a Saturday morning, we attended the Mayor's 'At Home' in the parlour at the Town Hall. Hundreds of performers flocked to Blackpool to entertain the holiday crowds and all were invited to come to meet the Mayor and each other socially on a Saturday morning. It was our job to greet the visitors at the top of the stairs, make them feel welcome and take them into the Mayor's parlour. Such well known personalities of the day as Ann Shelton and Wee Georgie Wood were among the visitors. Sometimes we had the opportunity to chat privately with the entertainers and we were reminded that outward success and recognition were certainly no guarantee of inner contentment and peace of heart. On a much more flippant note, on these Saturday mornings we also discovered the art of making one glass of orange juice last for hours!

I myself had the opportunity to become something of an entertainer at this time. I was chatting with a young bridegroom to be in the vestry before his wedding and I discovered that he performed as a conjuror in his spare time. The young man, Tom Owen, said that, as a thank you for conducting his wedding ceremony, he would be delighted to teach me a few tricks. He was true to his word: a month later he took me on. I proved to be a much better pupil at conjuring than I had been at maths or Latin! It was not long, thanks to Tom Owen, that I gained entry to the Magic Circle. Many is the time since that I have been able to combine conjuring and preaching the Gospel. A trick or two makes for a receptive audience!

Seven years into our stay at Blackpool we received two lovely gifts. We had been in our rented accommodation since our arrival, but now the church was in a position to purchase a vicarage. Our good friend Harold Grimbledeston, sold his house to the church; improvements were made and, at last, St. Mark's, Layton, had its own magnificent vicarage. The second gift was a personal one: a beautiful new Austin A30 car. Until now my parish rounds had been achieved on a 250 cc BSA motor bike, but the doctor advised me that, due to a kidney weakness, I would be unwise to continue travelling that way in all weathers. I was ready to take to the much more restricted life of a pedestrian but Christian friends in our congregation, George and Edith Frost, had other ideas. A garage telephoned me one day to inform me that my car was ready for collection. I protested that there must be some mistake. Then the story of the Frosts' wonderful generosity was revealed. What a luxury – my own car! What Olive and I did not know then of course was that the A30 was not going to see us round the roads of Blackpool for very long. But it would take us thousands of miles all over the British Isles in the years to come. It was, in fact, to wear itself out in a travelling ministry.

8: Call and Answer

A knock at the door soon after we had moved into our new vicarage was the start of our new way of life. There stood a lean young man who introduced himself as Bill Flagg, a South American Missionary Society worker home on furlough from Chile. Bill was living with his family in the parish and was due to return to Paraguay where he would be ordained. He wondered if I could provide him with experience of taking services and helping with church activities. Of course I was delighted to help. I knew virtually nothing at all about SAMS except that my old college friend Arthur Goodwin Hudson was connected with it. Apparently the Society was slowly emerging from a long period in the doldrums. Bill emphasised the need for an active Metropolitan Area Secretary to work on the Society's behalf at home. When we finally saw Bill and his family off to South America, he asked me prayerfully to consider whether I might be the man for the job.

Olive and I were far from eager to leave Blackpool. We had only just moved into the vicarage and I was adamant that we could not consider a move for at least a year. But we promised Bill we would pray. I then felt led to invite my friend Goodwin Hudson to Blackpool to lead an evangelistic campaign; at that time he was combining his work as part-time honorary General Secretary of SAMS with being incumbent of a London suburban parish. There followed an outstanding week of mission with many conversions. And while Arthur and his wife Elena were guests at the vicarage, Olive and I learned more about the work – and the potential – of SAMS. At the end of the week Arthur Goodwin Hudson too spoke of the Society's need for a Metropolitan Area Secretary. He asked me seriously to consider becoming a member of the SAMS home staff in London. Again I stated my reservations but suggested he contact me again in a year's time if the need remained.

So it was that, one year later, I found myself on the train to London to be interviewed by members of the SAMS General Committee with a view to joining the home staff. As I entered the room, the Chairman, Major W.F. (Bill) Batt, exclaimed discomfortingly, 'Oh, it's *you* is it!' – a remark that could have been interpreted in a number of ways! We had met briefly at a weekend houseparty in Lancaster and he remembered me from that. I was offered the post of Metropolitan Area Secretary in April, 1959. I had never in my wildest dreams anticipated doing such a job, but we sensed God's firm and persistent leading. Olive and I had promised Bill Flagg that we would pray – and we had. As we prayed and the post was not filled, the day came when we realised I was the one to fill it. Olive backed me all the way. We envisaged huge practical difficulties ahead, not least that both our children had reached a crucial stage in their education. But we had the Lord's clear call and we rested in His faithfulness.

If the parting from Lowestoft had been painful, the parting from Blackpool was doubly so. The final PCC meeting at which I announced my future plans was charged with emotion on both sides. There was a long silence and I was thankful when the moment came for me to vacate the chair and for my beloved friend Will Doxey to take over and discuss the future of St. Mark's, Layton, without me. So many familiar faces lined the road as we finally departed from the church in July,

1959. It was an unforgettable and emotional journey away from all we knew and loved. But, above it all, we sensed God with us.

My arrival in the SAMS office on the first day of August 1959 could not have been in greater contrast. 20, John Street, the Society's headquarters, was an old house and its interior had a distinctly Dickensian appearance and atmosphere. I had received a letter from Arthur Goodwin Hudson apologising that he was unable to be around to welcome me and listing the jobs that needed to be done. I knew two ladies should be at work on the premises, so I went first to find Miss Irene Watker who for many years had served as the Society's Financial Secretary and as secretary to Arthur Goodwin Hudson in his SAMS capacity. Miss Watker greeted me courteously and cautiously and handed me some keys which I would need to gain access to my office. She expressed the hope that I would be happy in my new work. Then I sought Miss Ethel Emery who looked after the visual aids and deputation side of the work. 'So you must be Harry Sutton!' she said warily looking up from her typewriter. She hoped we would be able to work happily together. The two ladies had held the fort at 20, John Street for several years and the arrival on the scene of an extrovert Lancastrian clergyman who was a complete stranger and who knew far less about the South American Missionary Society than they did, was understandably a cause for some reservation.

I made my lonely way up the winding stairs and located the door which I understood led to my office. I fumbled to find the right key and, when the door opened, I had the shock of my life. I had already sensed a Dickensian atmosphere about the place: this was surely Miss Haversham's room, but I was too taken aback at the time to think about the Great Expectations I had for my new job! I could not imagine that the room had ever been dusted, and it was cluttered with old

South American Indian relics from the mission field. My next move was instinctive rather than calculated, but it was a wise one. I sank down and prayed. I needed God's assurance that this was *really* the place for me.

A day or two later a dear friend from Liverpool called unexpectedly to see me. Having been a regular visitor to our vicarages in Lowestoft and Blackpool he found my new circumstances frankly unbelievable. As I saw him off down the winding stairs, I have a vivid recollection of his parting comment which shook me to the core: 'What a terrible waste of good manpower!'

Meanwhile, at home Olive was having to make major adjustments too. From being very much the mother figure who was deeply immersed in the ministry at Blackpool, she had become a housewife whose husband worked office hours and who would be away many weekends too. We hardly knew the south of England at all, let alone the Metropolitan Area which I was due to cover. SAMS had bought a pleasant, semi-detached house for us in Firs Walk, Woodford Green, so that we were living in Arthur Goodwin Hudson's parish of All Saints', Woodford Wells. The church and neighbours made us welcome but it was all very strange. We were especially grateful that the way opened up for Janet and John to attend good schools in the area, but the move to London meant a substantial drop in our standard of living and it was hard. Still, we were quite confident that this was God's place for us.

Hearing about the condition of my office, it was not long before Olive came with me equipped with cleaning materials. She unearthed all sorts of antiquated relics, magic lantern slides and curios which epitomised the missionary thrust of the past. She got the shock of her life one day when a life size model of an Araucanian Indian toppled out of a dark cupboard on top of her. One of our area secretaries pounced on this 'new' visual aid with relish and became a hazard on the road when he travelled to meetings with the Indian strapped to his roof rack!

Soon I was ready to begin serious work. I decided to write to about two hundred clergy in the London area, some of whom might know my name through NYLC or other evangelistic activities. Others, I felt, might be ready to support the Society if an opening were made. I also set about typing and duplicating the Society's prayer letter to its hundreds of praying partners. My office experience was very rusty by now and I received dozens of letters back complaining about the poor standard of the work. But, to my astonishment, I also received dozens of replies from the clergy saying they would be pleased to have me preach on behalf of SAMS. Since there are only fifty two weekends in the year, this meant that my Sundays were already fully committed for two years ahead.

My first deputation Sunday in August 1959 was at Morden Parish Church where Canon Tom Livermore was Rector. I took Harvest as my theme and based it on the text, 'The harvest truly is plenteous, but the labourers are few; pray ye therefore the Lord of the harvest, that He will send forth labourers into His harvest.' (Matthew 9: 37, 38). Arthur Goodwin Hudson had used the title 'Hindered Harvest' for his first address when he took over as General Secretary of SAMS. Fred Train, the key missionary in Paraguay at that time, wrote home, 'Let us face this serious fact that God's harvest is wasting through lack of harvesters.' Likewise Henry Grubb in Argentina had used the same image during the period after the war years, 'There have been great hindrances to the harvest of souls.' Unlike these men, I had no first hand knowledge, but I sensed what a vast harvest field for God South America proffered. Most Republics, of course, were nominally Roman Catholic, but Communism, secularism, humanism, animism and innumerable heretical sects were all seeking to reap that harvest. Ambassadors for Christ needed to arrive speedily on the scene, so my message at Morden that first Sunday emphasised the urgency of the situation in Latin America. There was a vital need for dedicated young Christian men and women to go as harvesters because the potential harvest of millions of souls was there for the reaping.

I realised that my contribution to the work of spreading the Gospel in South America was undoubtedly best made out and about in the parishes, promoting interest in the work of SAMS and encouraging practical and prayerful support. Apart from preaching in different churches each Sunday, I often found myself addressing midweek women's meetings. I always associate these in my memory with our Threepenny Bit savings card. There was a fascination about saving these little twelve-sided coins, twenty of which could be pressed into one card. I must have distributed thousands of them and they were a valuable source of income for the church overseas.

As the weeks went by, I became more and more aware that I was part of an exciting work of God. I captured something of the vision that had inspired magnificent men and women of God for over a century to give their lives to Him for service in Latin America. A naval captain, Allen Gardiner, had founded the Society in 1844 and gradually, over the years, a missionary work had become established in the republics of Chile, Argentina and Paraguay, but purely among the indigenous Indian tribes. After flourishing until the 1930s, the work suffered severely as a result of World War Two. There were no reinforcements to missionary personnel or opportunities for furlough in England. The indigenous Indian churches were quite strong by now, but by no means ready for independence. A new initiative was required to get the Society on the move again in the post war years and it was Arthur Goodwin

Hudson whom God used to do it.

While I was a curate in Toxteth and Bebington, Arthur Goodwin Hudson was serving as Chaplain to the English-speaking community in Santiago, Chile. It was not easy. The Bishop in South America at that time disliked an evangelical emphasis and urgently tried to dissuade him from trying to stir up the dying embers of SAMS. But Goodwin Hudson returned home with a clear and determined vision and he became the Society's part-time General Secretary in 1948. I have no doubt whatever in my mind that God used him to save the South American Missionary Society from extinction. By the time I arrived on the scene a decade later, some key reinforcements had been made to missionary personnel including, of course, Bill Flagg. The General Committee at home too had been strengthened. The Chairman was now Major Bill Batt and the Treasurer was Colonel Tony Kimpton. Both were outstanding Christian laymen.

I did not keep my job as Metropolitan Area Secretary for long. In December 1959, Olive and I strayed out of our area back to Liverpool on deputation. We bought a Christmas tree in Paddy's market before making the slow return journey home down the old A6. There was a big pile of mail on the mat when we arrived and among the Christmas post was a personally delivered envelope bearing Arthur Goodwin Hudson's handwriting. The letter informed me that he had been appointed Coadjutor Bishop of Sydney in Australia.

It was not long before the General Committee asked me if I would be prepared to become the Society's Home Secretary with responsibility for the whole of Great Britain. I accepted without hesitation. And my promotion did not stop there! In the Spring of 1960 the Committee decided that the time had come to appoint a full-time, paid General Secretary and up to a dozen men were interviewed. Days passed and I was called into a committee meeting and told that they were thinking of making an appointment. I said I would be ready to support whoever it was they had appointed. They burst into laughter and Major Batt asked me if I would accept the job! I accepted with joy, but with reservations too. I believed the appointment had God's approval, but I was very conscious of my shortcomings. So, I think, were the committee! As General Secretary, I would have to meet and negotiate with the hierarchy of the Church of England and also with academics at general missionary conferences. Even worse perhaps, I had no missionary experience whatsoever. Despite these handicaps however, the committee felt I was the man for the job and I was not going to argue with them!

Before he set off for Australia, Bishop Goodwin Hudson shared with me some of the encouragements and the disappointments of his decade with SAMS. Undoubtedly he was delighted that a new interest in the work of the Society had been aroused at home and the work was on the move again in South America. But it had been his great ambition to see the work extending into the towns and cities of the great continent. He did not wish to underestimate the importance of the Indian work, but he longed to see influential men and women in the cities too won for Christ and assuming positions of responsibility. This was a vision I understood and shared. But there were several members of the Committee at home and, more important, the missionary team abroad, who feared that an extension to the cities would be a betrayal of the Indians and would inevitably mean a weakening of the work among them. It was a critical issue and one that was going to have to be worked out in the coming years.

Plunged suddenly into the deliberations of the General Committee, from which I had been excluded until now, I found myself rather an outsider. But I was determined to have my say. I found it particularly disturbing that different missionaries on the field tended to write home with their proposals and grievances to various members of the committee, so that these letters came fresh to committee meetings for our consideration. I asked that all such correspondence should, in future, be addressed to me and I would ensure that duplicated copies were distributed to all members. Then we could all come to meetings informed and better prepared.

The Committee itself continued to be reinforced with first class, dedicated men and women of God. Among these were Major General Sir Arthur Dove and Admiral Sir Horace Law who, along with Major Batt and Colonel Kimpton, earned the comment that SAMS was fast becoming a second Salvation Army. We had no argument with that! I counted it a great privilege to work with these men. After serving as an officer in the Coldstream Guards, Major Bill Batt had returned home to farm the family estate at Gresham in Norfolk. The vicar of a neighbouring parish, the Reverend H.G. 'Hammy' Thompson, an Irish Protestant and a former missionary in China, longed to see Major Batt won for the Lord. The Major was a regular church goer and became increasingly aware that the Gospel of Jesus Christ demanded some sort of definite decision: either Jesus was who He said He was, in which case He deserved full allegiance, or He was not.

In 1932, the Major went with 'Hammy' Thompson to a mission in Norwich led by Bishop Linton of Persia. He was soundly converted and all the discipline and commitment characteristic of an army officer were transferred wholeheartedly to the cause of the Gospel. Major Batt believed very strongly that God wanted him to remain just where he was, convinced that a Christian in a responsible position can have a far reaching effect for Christ. And so it proved. He arranged for several evangelistic campaigns in his area of Norfolk and used his home, as he does to this day, as a lovely setting in which to introduce people to Christ. His main interest was the student world and he became especially involved with the Cambridge University Christian Union. By 1952, when he was first introduced to SAMS through contact with Arthur Goodwin Hudson, Major Batt was deeply committed to evangelistic work all over the country. An indefatigable man, he also served on forty different committees of which he was chairman of ten, and was a District Councillor, County Councillor, Alderman and Magistrate! When Goodwin Hudson asked if he would add the SAMS Committee to his list, he refused at first, but relented with the comment, 'I'll do it, but I don't know a thing about it!' Characteristically he did not remain in ignorance for long. And within a few months, during one of the few General Committee meetings he was unable to attend, he was elected Chairman in his absence!

In 1954 Colonel Tony Kimpton joined him as Treasurer. Unlike Major Batt Tony Kimpton had been converted as a child. He was no stranger to SAMS either because his mother, Mary Kimpton, was a keen supporter of the Society and held missionary garden parties at their home in Wallington. As a young man Tony Kimpton was an enthusiastic and energetic witness and is especially remembered in Christian circles as a founder member of the thriving Sutton Crusader Class. But later he entered a spiritual wilderness. He admits that his love of the world took precedence over his love for God. Many friends – and not least his wife Rachel – prayed for him during these years of backsliding. Their faithfulness was rewarded. Coming in very late one night after a Conservative party ball, he had a dramatic experience of God's presence, and surrendered his life afresh to Christ.

This experience coincided with the Billy Graham Crusade at Harringay and he took every opportunity to take his friends along and several were converted. Also at Harringay he met up with Major Batt who asked if he would consider joining the SAMS Committee. Colonel Kimpton became an outstanding supporter of the Society. He was also a founder member of the Directors' and Partners' Christian Union whose motto was 'The City for the Lord.' And he was instrumental in introducing the Rev Dick Lucas to St. Helen's, Bishopsgate.

Both Major Batt and Colonel Kimpton were to suffer tremendous personal loss in later years. Major Batt's elder son, Christopher, was killed in an air crash and Colonel Kimpton's daughter Patricia died in a road accident. But their Christian faith and assurance during these times of intense grief only revealed they were men of great spiritual calibre. Their contribution to the South American Missionary Society at a crucial time in its history cannot be overestimated.

Yet another wonderful friend appeared on the scene in 1960. The Rev. Robert Smith and his wife Dorothy had returned from serving with the Sudan United Mission in Africa and Robert had become vicar of a village near Blackburn when our paths first crossed. I went to address a diocesan evangelical fellowship in Preston and Robert was present. I suppose I was to Robert what Bill Flagg and Arthur Goodwin Hudson had been to me, and it was not long before he became SAMS North West Area Secretary. But more than that, Robert Smith was to be a beloved friend whose support and wise counsel in ensuing years was to be of such enrichment to me. Olive and I count our friendship with Robert and Dorothy as one of the great blessings of our life.

When, in the Spring of 1961, it was decided that I must go to South America to gain first hand experience of the Scoiety's work, I set off knowing that Robert would be holding the fort in the parishes at home. He moved with his family to live in Woodford Green. Olive and the children were now firmly rooted in Woodford and in the life and fellowship of All Saints' Church where Melville Scutt had succeeded Arthur Goodwin Hudson as Vicar. We rejoiced in God's continuing care.

9: Forward Move

It was a momentous day for me in June 1961 when I boarded the plane at Heathrow. This was my first journey outside Great Britain! But certainly not my last. When I arrived in Buenos Aires via Rio de Janeiro and then Montevideo in Uruguay, I was met by the private secretary of Bishop Daniel Ivor Evans whose vast diocese consisted of the Falkland Islands, Argentina, Paraguay, Uruguay, Chile, Bolivia and Peru. So all SAMS work at that time lay within it. The secretary handed me a letter from the Bishop welcoming me and requesting my presence in his office the following day.

I spent my first night in the City Hotel. I enjoyed one of the largest steaks I had ever seen, while recalling – with some sense of guilt – that malnutrition was rife among the Indians I was soon to meet.

It had been Bishop Daniel Evans who had made it clear to Arthur Goodwin Hudson that he would like to see an end to the work of SAMS in his diocese. The Bishop disliked our evangelical emphasis, feeling that it gave a false impression of Anglicanism in general. I was going to have to tread warily. At our meeting the first morning, the Bishop reached for his huge Book of Common Prayer and asked if I read it every day. I confessed that, although I read it regularly, I gave greater priority daily to reading the Bible. I have always believed the Bible to be God inspired, whereas the Prayer Book is the work of men. Our continued discussions only served to accentuate our differences.

As we parted, Bishop Evans insisted that I should report back to him before returning home. He wanted to know all the recommendations I would make to the Committee.

I was glad to move on to Chile and to meet the SAMS missionary team there. I was met in the capital, Santiago, by Douglas and Rosalind Milmine. It was hoped that the vision of those who wished to expand the Society's work into some of the great towns and cities of South America, would find fulfilment here. The Society had already bought a property known as 'The Centre' and Douglas and Ros Milmine were preparing to launch out on a Spanish speaking ministry which would be a major breakthrough in the Society's policy.

The Milmines accompanied me on the 450 mile journey from Santiago to the south of Chile where SAMS missionaries had been at work for sixty years in the fields of evangelism, medicine, education and agriculture. The work was strongest in the small towns surrounding the city of Temuco, like Cholchol and Quepe. Then it extended to the very rural areas inhabited by the Mapuche Indians.

The railway journey south took me into a new world. I found myself in the mixed culture of Mapuche Indian and Spanish speaking Chilean. The city of Temuco was a kaleidoscope of colour and a cauldron of activity. The open air and covered markets were fascinating – they were full of local handicrafts and bustling with life.

The Anglican Church in the area was still small but growing. A major problem we faced was how to train national Chilean leaders fast enough for the task that lay ahead. Tony Barratt, one of the fine missionary reinforcements of the fifties, had recently started a Bible Institute at Quepe with the aim of preparing and training national pastors and evangelists.

The few Chilean pastors already ordained were outstanding Christian men. It was not possible to pay them the wage they richly deserved so their domestic and social circumstances could only be described as very poor indeed. Their standard of living though was infinitely better than many of their church members. I was deeply impressed at the way these Chilean Indian Christians had a desire to share their faith with others. I had rarely seen this spontaneity in England. There was no discernible programme for evangelism, simply the urge to evangelise was enough. A valuable lesson there!

I loved Chile and very many different impressions and memories swirled in my mind as my first trip there came to an end and I prepared to fly back to Argentina. I found the extensive travelling bewildering and the contrast of culture utterly confusing. It was possible, within a relatively short journey, to step through 100 years of social history. But I had seen the potential of the work for Christ and went away determined to do all in my capabilities, under God, to see that the work was fully supported from home.

Before I set off for South America, a lot of criticism and disquiet had been expressed about the Society's out of date and unattractive visual aids which did little to help promote interest in SAMS at home. A very generous gift of £2,000 had been received especially for the purpose of updating this area of our work. It was discovered that Jim Normington, a fine cameraman who worked for the Church Missionary Society, could be spared for secondment to SAMS for six months and Jim travelled to South America while I was there, in order to put together two films on our work. Jim was an excellent travelling companion and, as we were to discover later, did an excellent job for us.

I was busy with my own camera too. It was the work of the people I primarily wished to record, but I was thankful not to miss one of the most outstanding views I have ever witnessed. The plane journey back over the Andes to Argentina was utterly breathtaking and awe inspiringly beautiful. I felt the profound privilege of being able to witness a scene of such grandeur in the course of my calling. The might of the Creator and the beauty of His creation cannot, surely, be more readily acknowledged than in the snowcapped peaks of the Andes.

I arrived back in Buenos Aires and then took a much smaller plane north to the somewhat primitive airfield in the small town of Oran in Northern Argentina. Francis Tompkins was there to meet me and he escorted me throughout my tour of what remained of the SAMS work in that republic. During the 1920s and 1930s the work among the Indians – evangelistic, educational and medical, had spread rapidly and mission stations had sprung up to meet a need all over the Chaco region. But few of them were occupied now, especially as one or two missionaries were home on furlough.

Entering the Chaco was a strange experience. I felt the utmost respect for those pioneer missionaries who had travelled this way alone on horseback. One moment we were in dense forest and the next in monotonous open scrubland; an incredible bounty of exotic birds added colour and variety. Travelling through the Argentine Chaco made such a deep impression on me that I could never be quite the same again. If I needed any extra incentive to further the work of SAMS in Latin America, I received it then. Both the poverty of the people and the courage of the little Christian community had to be seen to be believed.

I was acutely conscious too of the sacrifices made by the missionaries and their children. I almost felt afraid for them. Apart from the emotional stress of living amid such squalor, the stifling heat, the flies, the bugs, the lack of adequate diet meant that so much of their time was taken up with the basic art of survival. Travelling too was always hazardous. In winter the roads were mud tracks through the forest, into which wheel axles slipped and stuck. In the summer they were dust tracks. A thick dry, choking dust blew everywhere, enveloping the vehicles and their passengers.

I vividly recall after one weary day's travel, arriving at a little mission house which had been empty for some time. We were to spend the night there and, as we pushed open the door, I was overwhelmed by the stench of inches of bat droppings. It was awful – yet my companions took it all in their stride. In contrast I also vividly remember the great relief I felt, a few days later, to be greeted by Aphra Ward and Helen Sohns in another remote mission house. The sight of two ladies plus one or two home comforts was more welcome than I can say!

A clear pattern for the future emerged as my time in Northern Argentina drew to a close. The programme of direct evangelism and church building must continue. But it was clear that a new and enlarged medical work, together with intensive agricultural projects, was urgently required. I was appalled to see at first hand the effects of widespread malnutrition. Never shall I forget the experience of attending the funeral of the baby of a Christian Indian family who had died as a result of malnutrition. If ever I needed encouragement to go back to Britain and continue my work for SAMS, my visit to Northern Argentina provided it. I knew that Christian mission was going to consume my life from now on.

At the end of my stay in Northern Argentina, Derek Hawksbee came all the way from Paraguay to accompany me on my journey to the Paraguayan Chaco. This was the area that one of the great SAMS pioneer missionaries, Barbrooke Grubb, had fearlessly opened up over sixty years previously. It is believed Grubb was the first white man to reach the interior of the Paraguayan Chaco and come out again. For reasons not easily defined, the Anglican Church had been slower to take root in the Paraguayan, as opposed to the Argentine, Chaco. Nevertheless there was a real spiritual quality in the indigenous Indian Church, nurtured by a few national pastors and evangelists.

The work was centred on the original mission station at Makthlawaiya, an island in the middle of a swamp. Here the little church flourished among the Lengua Indians. Then, in the late fifties, Dorothea Wedgwood and Jocelyn Padbury had left our home church in Woodford Green to establish a school for the Lenguas and some Spanish speaking children whose parents, mainly ranchers, worked on Makthlawaiya. This was already having a profound effect on the children both spiritually and intellectually. There was a dispensary too, but no qualified medical missionary to administer it.

Here again I was deeply impressed by the dedication of the missionaries. What a contrast to the life they had left behind! Mosquitoes, flies, bugs and intense heat made life almost unbearable for the uninitiated. And it was so difficult to sleep at night: I could cope with the steady drone of traffic from the nearby A11 when home in Woodford, but the uncanny noise of the frogs and other nightlife in the Paraguayan Chaco kept any restful sleep at bay. I could not catch up on sleep in the early hours of the morning either: a dozen or more cockerels crowed lustily at first light and expected everyone else to show similar enthusiasm for greeting a new day!

As a visitor I was given the best food the missionaries had to offer and I was always grateful. But I was not deceived. I knew the sort of meals we were eating were exceptions rather than the rule. The normal mediocre diet lacked variety. I still recall with great pleasure the relief and joy it was each evening to be welcomed into the home of Derek and Betty Hawksbee after a day out and about in the Paraguayan Chaco. We would tune in to the BBC Overseas Service to hear the News and it seemed so unreal to hear the chimes of Big Ben in this remote place.

Next I travelled to the capital city of Asuncion. My journey by plane took eighty minutes: the missionaries usually travelled by bullock cart and took several days. 60% of Paraguay's population live in the capital city and our missionaries, Bill and Marjorie Flagg, were settling down to a ministry there. Bill was Chaplain to the English speaking church of St. Andrew but, like the Milmines in Santiago, he was hoping to open up a Spanish speaking ministry too.

The way ahead in Paraguay seemed clear. We must consolidate the excellent, if small, evangelistic, educational and medical outreach at Makthlawaiya and aim to develop the Spanish speaking work in Asuncion. With more manpower it was hoped that a move could soon be made into Paraguay's second city, Concepcion, and also some of the capital's suburbs.

By the end of my tour, I was exhausted and confused, but thoroughly stimulated by the tremendous potential of our work. In my excitement, as soon as I arrived in Buenos Aires again on the first stage of my journey home, I impetuously sent a telegram to Tony Barratt, Douglas Milmine and Bill Flagg asking them to meet me so that we could finalise in detail our united recommendations for the future. And after that happy time together I reported back to Bishop Evans.

Understandably the Bishop was extremely angry that I had called three leading clergymen to Buenos Aires without consulting him first or, indeed, including him in our consultations. We had no right to discuss mission affairs as though they were separate from diocesan affairs, he said. That was my first serious blunder as General Secretary of SAMS, due entirely to lack of experience. I tried to make peace but sadly the rift between us had widened and the seeds of tension between mission and established church had become more deeply implanted. I had the utmost respect for Bishop Evans whose beliefs, however different from mine, were honestly and sincerely held. I was extremely sorry for my indiscretion.

Back home! There was an emotional reunion with Olive, Janet and John, then back to the office to commit to paper the many vivid impressions imprinted firmly in my mind and on my heart. I submitted a report to the General Committee so that the plans and hopes of those on the Field could be implemented as soon as possible. The outcome was to plan a bold Forward Move. Initially it was aimed to last three years in which we would recruit and send out forty five new missionaries. We resolved to strengthen and extend all the Indian work already in existence and to see the work in Santiago, Chile, and Asuncion, Paraguay, established and expanded to cover further cities and suburbs. Major Batt was especially keen to see a witness established among the University students of Latin America: potential future leaders as he saw them.

To launch our Forward Move, we prepared an informative, attractive brochure which was sent to every parish in the British Isles. Jim Normington's films too played an invaluable part in helping to portray the great needs and opportunities for the Gospel in Latin America. 'Foothold in the Andes' showed the work in Southern Chile, and 'Chaco Mission' highlighted the work among the Indians of the Paraguayan Chaco and between the rivers Pilcomayo and Bermejo in Northern Argentina. The films were very soon much in demand by parish churches; in a way they symbolised our intention to go forward and to meet the challenge of a new decade.

About this time, a young BBC technician phoned me and introduced himself as Len Thompson. Len was keen to use his professional skills in his spare time to promote the work of spreading the Gospel overseas. I was not going to pass by the offer of such specialised help – so we got together and 'pioneered' a regular prayer tape ministry. Len compiled prayer tapes using up to date news and prayer requests recorded by missionaries on the Field; then, with the help of his wife Brenda, the tapes were sent out bi-monthly to as many as a hundred different praying groups around the country. This of course was in the days of cumbersome tape recorders and tape reels, and it was a time consuming, dedicated labour of love. It was also of immense value to SAMS' Forward Move.

With the increased activity, the winding staircase at 20, John Street, began to take more wear and tear than it had for many years! But just as the Forward Move was gathering momentum I was stopped in my tracks. The date was Saturday, May 6, 1962. I had driven to John Street to have a preliminary interview with a couple who had offered themselves for service with the Society. I felt rather tired but otherwise quite well. During the interview I was conscious of niggling pains in my chest but put it down to indigestion. On my way home the pain intensified dramatically. Olive immediately sensed that something was very wrong and sent for the doctor who rushed me off to our little local hospital, the Jubilee. There I was told I had suffered a serious heart attack.

The Matron warned me that I must remain virtually immobile. I could not even clean my own teeth! I was devastated. SAMS had launched a bold Forward Move in which I so enjoyed being the front runner, yet the Lord had allowed me to be laid helplessly on the sidelines.

I missed the SAMS Annual General Meeting that year. I later learned that, in his address, Major Batt, using characteristic military images, had likened our work to warfare. We were on Christ's side in a battle for souls in South America. The going was tough but we were gaining ground. However, there had been one war casualty who had been forced to withdraw his services for a while. I had not looked upon my illness in this light before and, had I known what the Major was saying as I lay helplessly in bed, I think I would have appreciated a little more sympathy!

As I slowly recovered I found a ministry in the hospital ward, talking to the other patients. Indeed, once the activities of the day were over, some would bring their evening drink over to my bed and talk of their problems and needs. I was asked to end our time together with a prayer before we settled down for the night. I felt privileged to be able to testify to the love of God and the power of Christ in our little local hospital. And I know that one or two of the men made a definite commitment to Christ.

I received very many letters and cards of warm encouragement. None spoke more significantly to me than one from Henry Grubb who had served the Lord so faithfully in the Argentine and Bolivian Chaco but who had now retired to Norfolk. One sentence in particular stood out: 'However careful you are after this heart attack, your life will never be the same.' In fact, after ten weeks in hospital, my doctor encouraged me to live as normal a life as possible and not to consider myself an invalid. But Henry Grubb was right: life would never be the same again. God had healed me but He had also brought home to me the frailty of life. I was far more conscious of the nearness of eternity, of my total dependence on Him and of the urgency of preaching the Gospel.

An exhilarating, refreshing holiday at Chateau D'Oex in Switzerland put the final touches to my healing. When the Autumn arrived, I was ready to re-enter the field of battle!

10: Decade of Discovery

Once fit again, I was soon off on my travels. In January 1963 I flew to Latin America this time to represent SAMS at an important consultation convened by Bishop Stephen Bayne of the USA. The Archbishop of Canterbury's liaison officer, it was Bishop Bayne's job to co-ordinate the work of the Anglican Church around the world. The fact that the Anglican Church had committed itself to a greater involvement in Latin America, not least through SAMS, was obviously part of his responsibility because the vast South American diocese of the Falkland Islands, Argentina, Paraguay, Uruguay, Chile, Bolivia and Peru, was, still, at that time, an Extra Provincial Diocese of Lambeth.

Things had changed however. A few months previously we had been shocked to learn that Bishop Daniel Evans had met with a fatal accident on a bus journey in Chile. The Bishop had not yet been replaced. There were many others who shared his view that SAMS should not be allowed to expand too freely unless the balance was redressed by representation of other types of churchmanship within the Anglican Communion. Thus the Consultation on 'The Anglican Communion and Latin America' had been convened in Cuarnavaca, Mexico, where all interested parties could be represented. Dr. Donald Coggan, the Archbishop of York was appointed Chairman.

But, as far as SAMS was concerned, the Consultation turned out to be rather like a court case with the key witness missing. It was generally agreed that the base of Anglican churchmanship in Latin America should be broadened, but there were no specific recommendations as to how this might come about. It was decided that, for the time being anyway, the Anglican commitment should remain with SAMS.

One most important outcome of the Cuernavaca Consultation was that the large, unwieldy diocese which covered one sixteenth of the earth's surface would be divided into two as it had before 1937. One diocese was to serve Argentina and Eastern South America with the Falkland Islands; the other, Chile, Bolivia and Peru. I was still in South America when Colonel Kimpton phoned from London with the names of the two new Bishops: Cyril Tucker, Vicar of Holy Trinity, Cambridge, was to be the Bishop of the Eastern diocese and Kenneth Howell, who had served as a SAMS missionary in Chile for a decade from 1937–47, was to be Bishop of Chile, Bolivia and Peru.

SAMS was not consulted at all in the appointments and, for this reason, some members of our Committee were reluctant to meet with the Archbishop of Canterbury's request that the Society should contribute substantially to financing the two new dioceses. But I was among those who felt strongly that we must co-operate in any way we could. We thus agreed to pay for the passage of the two Bishops out to South America and a considerable sum towards their salaries.

The formation of the two dioceses meant a new and different situation for our missionaries. Their loyalty was above all to God, but they now had three other voices to whom they must listen: their own national Church which was becoming stronger daily, the Society at home, and the diocesan Bishop. In London we may have been a long way from the action, but it was our responsibility to remain as sensitively in tune as possible.

So the '60s became a decade of delicate negotiation between National Church, established Church and Mission. It was time for SAMS to be ready to hand over authority, property and land, learning to be the servant of a National Church rather than a domineering overseer. There were tensions and difficulties, but we *were* able to learn from the experience of the Church in Africa and India which had already undergone this transition. Like any parent, it was thrilling to see our child, the national Church, gaining more independence and growing stronger, but it was difficult to feel we were no longer totally indispensable. There were, of course, key areas in evangelism, education, medicine and agriculture where SAMS recruits were still vitally in demand, but we needed to be constantly sensitive to see where our true role lay.

Under God, our first Forward Move fulfilled most of its objectives. By 1963 the number of missionaries had risen to eighty and our income had increased from £26,000 to £62,000 within the three year span. That success only made us more determined to do even greater things for God. We had our critics who felt that any advance we had made as a Society was just part and parcel of the 'we've never had it so good' climate of the decade and that we would run out of steam. Nevertheless I have always maintained that we were privileged to be wrapped up in a real work of God. He brought together at that time all sorts of circumstances and agencies, of which SAMS was just one small part, so that His Holy Spirit could move in a special way throughout the Continent of Latin America.

The growth of the Christian Church throughout the Continent was – and indeed continues to be – phenomenal. At ten per cent it even exceeds the growth in population. The Pentecostal Church in particular has grown at an astonishing rate. In comparison, the growth of the Anglican Church is very small, but it *has* been significant. I believe Anglicanism has its part to play as an interpreter between the traditional Roman Catholic Church on the one hand and the new Pentecostal movement on the other; the kind of Anglicanism represented by SAMS is middle ground, understanding both extremes and to some extent identifying with both, so that we are able to interpret one to the other.

Within this great movement of the Spirit of God there were other specific reasons for the Society's own resurgence. The Lambeth Conference of Bishops from the worldwide Anglican Communion had in 1958 declared in its report, 'South America offers a challenge and opportunity to the Anglican Communion as a great field for evangelistic work. There is every reason why it should assume larger responsibilities there.' It was only SAMS which took up the 'challenge and opportunity' so any interest in, or enthusiasm for, extending the work of the Church in Latin America was channelled through us. In fact the Church at home was looking for a new part of the world in which to become involved now that the churches in the great Continents of Africa and India had, as it were, come of age.

Also history has now endorsed what many had always maintained – that the Billy Graham Evangelistic Campaigns in the Fifties had had a significant impact on the Church in Britain. There were thousands of converts, the majority of them genuine and lasting. Many of these were ready and trained by the time of our Forward Move to go out and win others. Latin America was brought to their attention as 'the Continent of opportunity', an attractive spiritual challenge. Some therefore who felt God was calling them to service overseas became SAMS recruits and ultimately first class missionaries.

The Charismatic Movement was also beginning to gain ground in the '60s. I think it is true to say that some young people who were open to God the Holy Spirit in a new way felt more 'at home' with SAMS than they did within a more traditional setting. The whole Latin American environment lent itself to a freer expression of faith and worship.

As the '60s progressed and it became apparent that SAMS was here to stay and its upsurge was not just a flash in the pan, the possibility of a merger with other missionary societies began to arise. In particular, my old friend from student days, James Seddon, who was now Home Secretary of the Bible Churchmen's Missionary Society, felt that there could be considerable advantages in a merger between his society and ours.

I myself was not in favour of a merger, but I was very ready to listen to the pros and cons as expressed by someone as experienced in the world of mission as Jim. I knew that a merger of the two societies could well strengthen the evangelical cause at home, but I was doubtful that it would help the small, but fast growing Church in Latin America. On a practical level, I knew that missionary societies which had merged in the USA could teach us some interesting lessons. Surprisingly, perhaps, they had also demonstrated that there were no financial advantages. In fact, it costs more to run one large society than it does to run several smaller ones working independently.

Following our informal meeting, a day conference was planned at Church House, Westminster, when members of both General Committees could air the issues. For me, it turned out to be a sad occasion. The main desire of those who spoke most was to preserve the status quo without considering any of the possibilities of a larger, united missionary society. The outcome was that we decided to shelve the possibility for the time being. It was not this that disappointed me but rather the unhelpful and negative approach of some of those present. Nevertheless I continued to be in close personal fellowship with Canon A.T. Houghton, the General Secretary of BCMS, one of the greatest evangelical missionary statesmen, and Jim Seddon.

Critics of SAMS of whom there was never a shortage, accused us of lacking clear cut policy and of allowing events to overtake us and to dictate the direction in which we should go. There was an element of truth in this criticism but it was by no means wholly justified. For example, there were 'The Gresham Conversations'. When such senior missionaries as Bill Flagg, Derek Hawksbee, Tony Barratt and Douglas Milmine were home on furlough, we met together on several occasions at the home of our Chairman, Major Batt and his wife Elisabeth at Gresham Hall, near Sheringham in Norfolk. They were the most gracious hosts and we were able to spend long, undisturbed hours over several days, in prayer and consultation together as to the needs of the hour and the way ahead. The missionaries knew the situation on the Field and were in close touch with Bishop Tucker and Bishop Howell so that our discussions were always relevant. I think these 'Conversations' showed our responsibility in matching the growth of the Society to clearly defined needs overseas.

A follow up to the Consultation in Cuarnavaca was called in January 1966, this time in Sao Paulo, Brazil, in order to reassess the situation three years further on. Again Dr. Donald Coggan was our Chairman. The Sao Paulo Consultation reiterated what was said at Cuarnavaca, 'that our primary objective is the development of Latin American churches expressive of the genius of their own countries and of the unity of the Anglican Communion.' Again too it was resolved that there should be greater integration of all Anglican work under the direction of the diocesan Bishop. The outstanding growth of the Pentecostal Church was noted with pleasure and it was acknowledged that 'our own Church should be willing to learn from the Pentecostals and all other evangelical churches what God the Holy Spirit has been teaching them and achieving through them, and to serve them in any way that is open to us.' The South American Missionary Society had no quarrel with that. Our Forward Move continued.

But once again for me illness intervened. I found I had considerable difficulty in swallowing and X-rays revealed a Pharygial pouch which, if left untreated, would eventually choke me. I first underwent surgery at Guys Hospital in September 1964. But by the time I arrived back from the Sao Paulo consultation, it was clear that a further operation would be necessary. The pouch in my throat had reappeared, much larger this time.

After a second operation in April 1966, I left hospital unable to speak. I was warned that my vocal chords could have been seriously damaged by the surgery or they could just be badly bruised. It was a tremendous blow to me to have to come to terms with the fact that I might no longer have the use of speech. For weeks I spoke in a low, hoarse whisper and I sank into deep depression believing that my preaching ministry had come to an end. I have to confess that I became so bound up in myself that I reached the stage where I even found it difficult to communicate with God. The lessons I had learned during my heart attack of the need for total reliance on God and not on myself had become blunted and neglected through the busyness of an overcrowded diary.

Olive realised that I needed a complete break and we found sanctuary for a while at the vicarage of our friends, Ken and Norah White, who were then in the fenland parish of Ramsey St. Mary, near Peterborough. Walking round the garden one day with Olive, I somehow knew that God wanted her to pray for me. As she did so, the Lord touched my soul in a fresh and exciting way. In the low, hoarse voice I loathed so much, I poured my heart out to the Lord and asked His forgiveness and cleansing. And so very gently He reminded me that it was my heart He wanted, not just the gift of preaching that I thought I had. At last I reached the point where again I was ready to surrender myself 'just as I am.' I even reached the point of being willing to glorify His Name with my silence if necessary. For years God had had my preaching; now He had the preacher.

It was several weeks later that my daughter Janet, herself a trained nurse by now, brought me a cup of tea in bed. I uttered an automatic 'Thank you', and we realised that my voice sounded almost normal. My heart overflowed with love of God and my lips with praise. I returned chastened, but restored, to my ministry with SAMS.

11: On the Move

Some months before my illness I had been surprised to receive a letter from Canon John V. Taylor, then General Secretary of the Church Missionary Society, suggesting that SAMS and several other Anglican missionary societies, including BCMS, might consider joining them in the new, purpose built CMS headquarters being erected in London's Waterloo Road. The letter arrived when the possibility of a merger between smaller missionary societies was still pressing for attention and the idea of working under the same roof seemed a reasonable compromise.

This offer came at a time when our premises at 20, John Street, had run right down and required a vast sum of money spent on making them safe and habitable. Nevertheless there were some members of our committee who felt it would be a mistake to move, believing that SAMS would be embarking on a road leading to an ultimate loss of identity. There was much prayer and discussion for many months before the decision to move was taken at the very last moment. It was not a unanimous agreement and I found the indecision hard to bear. It was just as well perhaps that the hottest debate occurred while I was out of action in the summer of 1966. Once more, Robert Smith who was now strongly established as the Society's Home and Candidates' Secretary, took the brunt of responsibility during my absence.

My burden was further reduced when a Chartered

Accountant, Rodney Mann, came to join us and to help cope with the welcome problem of the ever increasing size of our income. The time had come for Irene Watker to retire. I was never a businessman and was quite unsuited to cope with the administrative and financial matters: we needed an expert on the job.

During the '60s our income rose from under £30,000 a year to well over £100,000. We were partnered too in large capital projects overseas with such agencies as Oxfam, Christian Aid and later Tear Fund. So it was a great blessing when Rodney agreed to set aside some years of his career to develop the accounting system. One of the things I value most when I recall my days in the SAMS office, is the sense of mutual understanding and respect Rodney, Robert and I had for each other's gifts. Our relationship was an excellent example of the joy of being able to 'bear one another's burdens'.

The day of the move eventually arrived in November. CMS could not have been more co-operative and as time passed they proved very gracious hosts. 157, Waterloo Road was purpose built for missionary society requirements. The old SAMS furniture which looked so at home in John Street looked somewhat archaic and cumbersome in its new, modern surroundings. The very heavy antique safe (which bore the scars from where Barbrooke Grubb had used it as a chopping surface for his wood while on furlough in 1896!) was most reluctant to be moved. When it *was* finally deposited in its new home, it refused all efforts to be opened until experts from Chubbs arrived!

SAMS also acquired new premises of its own in 1966. As the number of missionaries increased during the '60s we felt the need for a training centre for recruits. Once the need was made known, two friends of SAMS, Ted and Marjorie Jenkin, made a generous gift to the Society of a large, fully furnished house in Tunbridge Wells, Kent. It was named Allen Gardiner House after the founder. During the Autumn it was used as a training centre for recruits; during the rest of the year as a conference centre. Ted and Marjorie themselves became the first wardens. The gift of Allen Gardiner House was a timely one. With the rapid growth in our recruitment of missionaries, it was imperative that they should be prayerfully and carefully selected and trained. As Bishop Tucker and Bishop Howell began to see the work in their dioceses taking shape and direction, they had specific requests for the sort of missionary recruits they needed. It was therefore our responsibility to send out the right sort of people.

I never took part in the recruits' Selection Committee. I left it to those far better experienced than I. They met with potential recruits at Allen Gardiner House; after four or five days in residence together, the hopefuls returned home while the committee stayed on to pray and choose those they felt should be accepted unconditionally; those who needed further training or experience and those who, they believed, should reconsider their calling.

There was no lack of recruits. We were always faced with a dilemma: should we accept them and trust God to provide the money to support them? Or only accept those we knew we could afford to maintain on present income? Certainly some committee members, including the new Treasurer Leslie Leppard, an outstanding Christian and fine professional businessman, felt it was wrong to take on responsibility without having the support to hand. They sincerely believed that God led *through* the provision of money; they objected to our special appeals. But it is a fact that some churches only sent to us in response to an appeal; otherwise they imagined we were well provided for and sent their money elsewhere! This tension existed over many years. Wise stewardship is, of course, a matter for the individual Christian. There is no clear cut answer.

For a short period we made the mistake of sending out too many recruits at one time. This had an adverse effect on the recruits themselves; they needed time to adapt to the shock of a strange culture and a revolutionised way of life. There were not enough experienced missionaries available to help the newcomers. I fear that the result was a casualty or two, but at least it was not a mistake we repeated.

Another sign of SAMS' change of status was to be invited to take a larger share in the affairs of the central missionary bodies. As General Secretary I became involved with the Missionary and Ecumenical Council of the Church of England, the Church of England Evangelical Council, the Conference of British Missionary Societies and ultimately the World Council of Churches.

I must admit that not a few SAMS committee members had wondered how I would cope as General Secretary representing the Society in these circles. Their fears may well have been justified. Constant consultations and committee meetings too often brought out the worst in me; I frequently must have appeared belligerent and arrogant as I expressed my black and white views in distinctly grey areas. I was sometimes accused of being anti-intellectual, simplistic and extremist. In my defence I must say I felt that some of my colleagues had over intellectualised the concepts of mission, evangelism and salvation. My faith was – and is – firmly based on such texts as John 14: 6, 'Jesus said, "I am the Way, the Truth and the Life; no one comes to the Father *but by Me*." ' And especially on Acts 4: 11, 'There is salvation in no one else for there is *no other name* under heaven given among men by which we must be saved.' From these I conclude that Jesus is not just the best of several alternatives or a super-charged Ghandi. He is *the only* Saviour. I make no apologies for that. I especially recall a large poster at one of the missionary conferences depicting an emaciated Indian in a drought stricken setting. The caption read, 'Salvation begins here.' This, according to my understanding of Christ's teaching, I utterly repudiated. Salvation begins at Calvary and the focal point of Jesus Christ's mission is a man's soul. This is not to say that I do not wholeheartedly endorse every effort that is being made to demonstrate God's love for the world through the relief of human misery. Nonetheless full stomachs do not *necessarily* lead to redeemed souls. In the passionate expression of these views, I fear I did not always represent SAMS well. Sometimes I was not even supported by other evangelicals because I did not represent the evangelical point of view as graciously as I ought.

However my public ministry to every corner of the British Isles was a real source of satisfaction. As the '60s unfolded it grew beyond my wildest dreams. There were three dimensions to my ministry – straightforward deputation work for SAMS at parish church level; addressing conventions or rallies and holding parochial missions. Once I had started on my round of deputation engagements, my diary was quickly filled from end to end. The innumerable beds in which I slept – long, short, narrow, wide, hard, soft, smooth and lumpy – were a mixed blessing! After one particularly cold weekend when my breath almost froze in the bedroom, I learned that a hot water bottle was a vital piece of equipment for someone in my position. But the joys far outnumbered the hardships.

Looking back I think that a number of improvements could have been made in deputation work. For example, I often arrived in a parish where only the Vicar knew I was coming. I found it very sad too when I was warned that the congregations were bound to be down that Sunday. So dull and uninspiring had Missionary Sundays been in the past that many people in the congregation chose that day to visit relations! A leaflet introducing SAMS and myself in advance would, I think, have prepared the way for more attentive ears and hearts. It saddened me when I sensed I was caught up in the atmosphere of 'Just another of those boring old Missionary Sundays'. The news I had to bring was so stimulating and so encouraging!

Acts 14 records how the apostles returned to the local church and reported on what the Lord was doing elsewhere. The deputation speaker and missionaries home on leave follow this excellent precedent. Additionally I realised that in my deputation ministry I had a wonderful opportunity to be a Barnabas – an 'encourager' to those I visited, not least to the Vicar and vicarage families. The deputation ministry, despite its weaknesses, fulfils a vital role in maintaining interest in the worldwide Church and of sharing encouragement in the Lord's work.

Alongside my deputation ministry there developed a Convention work. I was asked to speak on the Keswick Convention platform and then at smaller 'Keswicks' all over the United Kingdom. I thoroughly enjoyed it and found it a source of great satisfaction. Other public engagements, in contrast, I found utterly frustrating. For example, there was the occasion in the Royal Albert Hall when Cliff Richard was the chief attraction and I was the closing speaker. There was a long briefing. I was told what I should say, how I should say it and for how long. We went over and over the timetable in preparation. But, as is so often the case with such rallies, I was eventually able to get up to speak twenty minutes after the time I was scheduled to stop! By then everybody was only thinking about the last train home! On other occasions when I was the closing speaker, what had gone before was so positively excruciating that the audience was long past wanting to listen to me – and I was long past feeling inspired to speak. I spent the evening feeling like a caged lion! As I had been warned to stay clear of unnecessary stress, I decided it would be wise to refuse most invitations to address these rallies, and that is what I did.

Finally, there was the opportunity for direct evangelism. I could easily have spent all my time in this way but my first priority lay with SAMS. I was aware that a parish mission lasting a week or ten days required hours of preliminary preparation and once a mission was under way there was no time at all for further preparation. I had to limit my acceptances accordingly.

In the last twenty years I have led almost fifty parochial missions in the British Isles alone. It is a great joy to receive letters from people worldwide who express their gratitude for being led to the Saviour. But although I believe that a Parish Mission or a Crusade has a part to play in evangelism, most valuable of all is well planned continuous parochial evangelism of which a week of mission is just a part. Ideally I would advocate a three or five year cycle of carefully, prayerfully planned evangelism within a parish. The mission itself would play a strategic part, but the preparation and follow up would be of equal importance. This, sadly, too often remains an ideal. The Vicar and his staff are already overworked with day to day demands and have not the resources in time or manpower to plan such a long term evangelistic programme. In some wealthier parts of the world, an additional full time member of staff is employed purely for evangelistic work. There is no doubt in my mind that a climactic parish mission – a hiccup in the church's routine – is far less effective than an ongoing programme.

Again I was to be stopped in my tracks by another severe illness. It happened in the middle of a SAMS Summer School in August 1969. I suffered a second heart attack. At first, I have shamefully to admit, the invaluable lessons learned during my other two serious illnesses eluded me; this, I felt, must surely herald the beginning of the end of my public ministry.

I remained in hospital for some weeks in Tunbridge Wells and allowed myself to become depressed. Again I was blessed with the prayers and goodwill messages of so many friends but this time a word from my collegue Derek Hawksbee, who had now joined the home staff of SAMS, particularly helped. Derek urged me to accept my situation as it was and to seek God in it. Yet again the Lord had to break down so many barriers before He could get through to me. By nature I am an extrovert, proud, professional and conscious of myself. God dealt severely with such sinfulness. I have to confess that my illnesses were of inestimable value to my innermost being, even if my body took a hammering in the process. I was an obstinate disciple.

Eventually I was well enough to return to the office. Cushioned and shielded by my colleagues, as well as wonderfully cared for by Olive and, yet again, forgiven and restored by an infinitely patient Lord, I discovered it was not the beginning of the end after all. Since then I have travelled over half a million miles in His glorious service!

12: Canon Missioner

Slowly but surely I began to take up the threads of my SAMS life again. But it was while on a trip to Carlisle I realised that at last major changes would have to be made in my life style. I knew at once that pains in my chest as I carried heavy cases were caused through angina, the almost inevitable outcome of two heart attacks. Later, on the way home from North Wales, the pain compelled me to stop in my tracks and sit on my cases until a porter came to the rescue.

It became increasingly obvious that I should have to resign as General Secretary of SAMS in order to take life a little easier. But what could have been a depressing time was in fact an encouraging one. On returning home from a deputation tour in Ireland, Olive and I were met at the airport by our son John and his girlfriend Jennet. Both were school teachers: John's main subjects being Religious Education and Physical Education and Jennet's Music and Drama. The previous week they had attended the SAMS Summer School in the Lake District led by Canon Fred Train, a wonderful saint of God who had spent many years in missionary service in Paraguay. Now John and Jennet broke the news that they felt the call of God to missionary service overseas. You can imagine how that thrilled us. Somehow too it seemed a further seal on my growing conviction that my term of office as General Secretary should end.

John and Jennet were married in 1974 and subsequently attended All Nations Christian College for their missionary training. Ultimately they became part of a small SAMS missionary team in Peru under Bill Flagg who was now Bishop. Meanwhile, it was agreed that I *should* resign. But I was urgently encouraged to remain with the Society in the role of Canon Missioner. My new role would enable me to conduct evangelistic campaigns in SAMS supporting churches, to address missionary conferences and to speak on behalf of the Society at public rallies both at home and overseas. It was made generously clear that I was to take such commitments at my own pace.

I have no doubt why I was able to cover half a million miles since with no serious setbacks in my health. So many people all over the world covenanted to pray for me daily and I received continuous strength through their loyal support. And of course I cannot put too high a premium on Olive's loving care. She now travelled with me everywhere – not only to look after me either, she studied Christian counselling and in an unofficial way embarked on a ministry of her own. That meant her companionship on travels had purpose and fulfilment.

I had no idea as I started out on this new ministry that I was going to be inundated with requests for help. But that is what happened. Invitations and requests poured in, not only from the four corners of the British Isles, but also from Switzerland, the States, Canada, Australia and New Zealand. A tour of the States in 1975 was especially eventful and I think significant in my ministry. I went as an observer to churches enjoying a period of rapid growth; SAMS wanted me to find the reasons for this growth and to advise on whether or not there were lessons for British churches.

Two churches I visited were particularly outstanding. One was the Church of the Redeemer in Houston, Texas. A local politician confirmed that only a few years earlier the church and area around it were run down to the point of dereliction. Then through the vision of its pastor, Graham Pulkingham, and consequent charismatic renewal, the whole place came alive to God. Jeffrey Schiffmayer had become pastor by the time of my visit when I joined a congregation of 2,000 at a Series Three Holy Communion service. This included testimonies, prophecy and prayer for healing. As the service closed I distinctly heard several folk say, 'What a pity it's all over'. Yet it had lasted for 2½ hours!

Once derelict houses close by were now beautiful dwellings with prices rising continually as people wanted to move into the vicinity. Several were operating on an extended family principle; two or three families were moving into one property and, while one worked as the breadwinner for all, the others would devote their energies to the church and its outreach.

A second outstanding, but quite different, church was the Calvary Chapel at Costa Mesa in California. On the Sunday I was there 2,500 people attended each of three services held throughout the day. The pastor, Chuck Smith, had no doubts why; his secret he said was simple: 'Find out how God wants to move, then go with Him'. It was his belief that when a building catches fire, a lot of people come to watch. So it was with his church, but they not only came to watch, they stayed and got involved. The Calvary Church also made a tremendous impact on the whole neighbourhood. A village had been created where dropouts could find rehabilitation. In a Christlike way they were loved and respected as *people*, and their natural gifts were encouraged so that they could return to society equipped to cope emotionally *and* professionally. And that was not all: the church also maintained a day school, a re-sale shop and a coffee house. A Gospel concert held every Saturday attracted thousands. Its missionary outreach was no less impressive, including the maintenance of a radio station in San Salvador. Gospel programmes were transmitted for eighteen hours every day. Finally, four music groups which travelled all over the USA were supplied by the church!

Impressed I may have been, but I was enough of a realist to know that much of this was not readily transferable to the British Isles. Culture and temperament are so very different. In Britain today, we tend to be withdrawn inside ourselves, observers rather than participants, and we find it difficult to respond enthusiastically to anything, including the Christian faith. Television has not helped – yet in the States television is a significant factor in the Christian ministry and it does not always seem to result in passive viewing. As long as you can pay the bill almost any religious body can stage a programme. So evangelicals have a unique opportunity to communicate the Gospel and in many cases do so with conviction and great skill. In Britain, however, religious TV and radio programmes are usually prepared and interpreted by an elite. As a result some of the more dynamic interpretations of the Christian faith in this country are not adequately or fairly reflected. If by inclination we are a nation of observers, there is little stimulus on the Christian scene to make us otherwise. I wonder what cable television will do for us!

The transferable lessons from the USA, or indeed any part of the world where the Church is growing are basic to the spread of the Christian Gospel anywhere. The Christian Church grows only where there is *inspired motivation*. The truth is that although there are many instances in the UK where growth is possible, there is a sad lack of desire for it.

Undoubtedly a significant proportion of church growth during recent years owes much to the Charismatic Movement. Some people are of the opinion that this movement can be explained wholly in terms of a revolt against an impotent form of traditionalism and establishment. If this is so, like most other movements of rebellion, we can now expect it to decline because the point has been made.

But I am not sure that this understanding of the Charismatic Movement is the right one, although it does certainly seem to have peaked. I do not consider it to be a revolt, but rather a rediscovery of old truths neglected by the established Church. First and foremost of course fresh attention has been given to the Person and work of the Holy Spirit. Where a church or an individual believer has become a bag of dried bones, the Holy Spirit has been invited in to bring a breath of new life.

Sadly, charismatic renewal has proved divisive in some churches. Individual Christians have claimed a dramatic infilling of the Holy Spirit which has made those who simply experience a quiet, daily walk with Christ, feel like second class Christians. Matters of temperament have been falsely elevated into issues of spirituality. On the other hand there are very many in our churches who do not want God to disturb their way of life or worship at all. To have their traditional form of worship disturbed by movement and noise and invaded by religious dance and clapping of hands is very distressing. Then there are others who genuinely disagree with the movement on biblical and theological grounds.

There has been no problem when the charismatic emphasis was introduced to a new church. The membership grew together – spontaneously and at the same pace. This was also true of downtown churches where congregations had dwindled to a handful. In such cases the Charismatic Movement has been a source of enrichment. Today some of our finest churches are charismatic churches where a small congregation was brought to new life through a rediscovery of the power and work of the Holy Spirit.

Personally, I welcomed with great joy the new vitality

I sensed in worship and the new enthusiasm which believers were showing for the things of God. However I had great difficulty in agreeing that before such vitality could come about there must be an experience of 'Baptism in the Holy Spirit'. I found no satisfactory evidence in the Scriptures to suggest that two separate experiences are necessary. At conversion I believe we are saved both from the consequences and the power of sin; the one experience is sufficient.

But most of all in the earliest days of the Charismatic Movement, I had grievous problems with the view that the gift of speaking in tongues was an indispensable sign of the fullness of the Spirit of God in a believer. My understanding of New Testament holiness is that *all* Christians are baptised in the Spirit at conversion. After that our daily closeness to Christ determines the extent to which we are filled with the Spirit day by day. Because some people's walk is much closer to Christ than others', it is possible for them to be more full of the Spirit than those who only keep a nodding acquaintance.

The fullness of the Spirit in the believer is demonstrated primarily by the spiritual and moral qualities outlined in Galatians 5. I believe it is God's will that every one of his children should be filled with His Spirit and should display such qualities in the pressures of everyday life. I do not however underestimate the importance of the gifts of the Spirit as outlined in 1 Corinthians 12. A manifestation of the gifts of the Spirit did not end with the Apostolic age. Alongside the moral qualities of Galatians 5, there is room for the use of the gifts of the Spirit within the local church for its strengthening and encouragement. In my opinion one of the most important contributions of the Charismatic Movement has been its fresh emphasis on miracles. I believe we should look expectantly to God for the unexpected. The trusting, expectant church will be a growing church.

I am also convinced that there is a direct link between church growth and the leaders within the local church. This fact is terrifying in its implications but is nonetheless borne out by experience. The Pastor or Vicar and those who surround him should be men and women of assurance and faith – like Caleb (Numbers 13) who, with the other spies, saw the same giants, walled cities and other obstacles as they approached the Promised Land, but who *believed* that God would empower them to break down the barriers and cut the giants down to size.

But that is not the same thing as believing that a church should be minister orientated. It is impossible for one man to cover the ground physically or to cope emotionally. So it is absolutely crucial that lay men and women should be drawn into a team, sharing some of the tasks which in the past have been expected of the pastor alone. Now this is where one American idea could take root: the American Church has initiated a scheme, in which local churches set up scholarship funds for the express purpose of sending some of their young people to Bible College. The intention is simple; when these trained young people return to their own churches they will be stronger spiritually and responsible leaders. It is the clear belief of most churches in the States that a church grows as its leadership grows, and, as well as sending young people to Bible College, frequent seminars on Church growth and leadership are held at parochial church level. So every member is made aware of his or her responsibility and many become equipped to act upon it.

A growing church must have clear goals. If it does not really know where it is going, it will end up in disarray. Goals, once set, should be within the capabilities of the resources available, otherwise frustration and disillusionment set in. Methods to assist growth too must be carefully and prayerfully geared to the local situation. Something that works well in one type of situation can be a dismal failure in another.

And it should go without saying that a church must not only grow numerically but also in spiritual calibre. It is dangerous to see one kind of growth without the other. I have known churches to die of introverted fellowship. On the other hand there must be a strong base so that those from outside who are won to Christ are welcomed into a warm and healthy body.

As Canon Missioner I was happy to receive several invitations to Australia from the SAMS Auxiliary there. The missionary scene in the Anglican Church throughout Australia is somewhat confusing to English eyes. The CMS, which is different in ethos to that in England, tends to dominate the scene, especially in New South Wales. Then there is the Australian Board of Missions which is very strong in Western Australia. It was with difficulty that SAMS managed to find a foothold at all on the Australian missionary scene. In human terms it was due principally to the efforts of the Rev. Allan Yuill, Rector of Holy Trinity, Sydney, and Chaplain to Archbishop Moule. Later on Greg Blaxland, a former missionary in Chile, became Secretary and a tour by Archdeacon Tony Barratt greatly enhanced the Society's prospects for recognition. Now there were about a dozen Australian missionaries in South America.

My role was twofold. One was to be an ambassador for SAMS wherever I had an opening. The second was to conduct evangelistic missions in SAMS supporting churches. I made three separate trips to Australia during the '70s and stayed in Perth, Adelaide, Melbourne, Sydney and Tasmania. Each state is geographically separated by thousands of miles and the churchmanship of each I found very different. One was distinctly Catholic, another a mixture of traditions, while Sydney in New South Wales was largely evangelical and strongly influenced by Moor Theological College. The diocese of Sydney has welcomed Billy Graham on several occasions.

Australia is of course a relatively young sub-continent and this is reflected in its religious life. There are very few long standing traditions. The Anglican Church is gradually losing the characteristics that mark its English origin and the day has passed when senior posts are occupied by Englishmen. I found that the hierarchy in the Australian Church did not appear to be so remote from the rank and file as in Britain. My impression too was that the voice of the layman was more readily heard.

At home in England I was closely involved with such bodies as the Church of England Evangelical Council (CEEC) whose chairman was Dr. John Stott. Members of the Council were drawn mainly from diocesan evangelical unions, evangelical missionary societies and theological colleges. Its aim was to keep members abreast of religious and political matters and discuss them together. Matters for consideration at General Synod level were given special attention so that the evangelical element in the church might speak with one voice.

It had become increasingly evident during the '50s and '60s that evangelicalism was no longer a minority party within the Church of England with the clearly defined doctrine and style of worship of the period between the two world wars. I have to confess that I had become increasingly *more* Protestant and evangelical in my understanding of the Christian faith as the years had gone by. Nothing has changed since: I still fervently adhere to the beliefs I have held since the day of my conversion. I believe the Bible to be the inspired Word of God and sufficient in all matters of doctrine. I find my daily Bible reading like a road down which God comes to meet me. The erosion of this point of view among some evangelicals today gives me cause for great concern. I also still believe that all men need to be saved through faith in Christ and there is *no other way* of salvation. And my understanding of the doctrine of the priesthood of all believers is clearer today than at any time during my ministry.

It concerned me that the CEEC tended, as do so many councils and committees, to become divorced from the body of evangelical Christians in the local churches. There were some lay representatives from parish churches on the Council, but never enough of them. The Council was in danger of becoming an elite, almost an end in itself. I was therefore delighted when it was proposed to hold a conference in Nottingham University in 1977 with the aim of restating evangelical beliefs. A similar conference at Keele University in 1967 had, in my opinion, weakened rather than strengthened the evangelical element in the Church of England. Now I hoped for more. But I came away from Nottingham disappointed. Far from evangelicalism being defined more precisely and accurately, I thought the definitions were vaguer than ever. Only one positive point emerged: the Chairman, John Stott, emphasised his position as one of the outstanding evangelicals of our day. To me he is a Charles Simeon of the 20th century. When John Stott wrote his book 'Christian Mission in the Modern World' a critic commented that the author had not changed one bit over the decades. I am sure he was right, and that is the strength, not the weakness, of the man.

The Nottingham Conference highlighted the fact that evangelicals were having a growing influence within the Church of England. A higher percentage of those offering for ordination were from evangelical churches.

Also evangelical clergy were breaking away from established traditions and were being offered and accepting non-evangelical livings. Senior posts as Bishops and Archdeacons were being occupied by evangelicals and the voice and writings of distinguished evangelical scholars was increasingly being given attention.

On reflection I am sad that the growth in influence of evangelicals in the Church has not resulted in a significant movement towards a more biblical and reformed position. On the contrary, the growth could be said to coincide with a decline in moral standards. We fail it seems to penetrate the working classes of Great Britain and our involvement in world mission too often lacks urgency. Saddest of all is the lack of deep, sacrificial commitment to Christ and His Church.

Of course not all is negative in our churches. There is much to encourage us too. There is an upsurge in the number of young married couples who are returning to church. Additionally the number of students and undergraduates who are won to Christ is on the increase. Family Services are flourishing and ethnic churches continue to prosper. But it is no good pretending that I am happy with the way things are going. I especially regret that the broadening of evangelicalism in the Church of England has brought about a wholly changed attitude to the Free Churches. So strong is the desire to enter into dialogue with the Anglo-Catholic and Roman Catholic Churches that the Free Churches seem to have been forgotten. I have always found myself more at home with the Free Churches than the Church of Rome. I am a true Protestant at heart and it is for this reason that if, as was highly unlikely, the Church of England had offered me preferment of any kind, I would have declined. I could never in any circumstances have worn vestments. I know some Christians have thought this the attitude of a bigot, but I could not compromise in any way on this issue.

I regarded it as a great honour when in 1974 I was invited to become President of the Evangelical Alliance. I was not at all sure that I was the right kind of man to follow such great evangelical leaders as Dr. John Laird and Dr. John Stott. However I was assured by Gordon Landreth, General Secretary, and Ernest Oliver, General Secretary of the Evangelical Missionary Alliance, that they wanted me to be myself. For over 130 years the E.A. has been a voice at interdenominational level for evangelical Christians. It has provided a platform from which evangelicals have been able to make their views known to a wider constituency than is possible from the local pulpit. Through evangelism, social action and co-ordination, the Alliance has demonstrated that evangelicals have a useful contribution to make to our Church and nation. The E.A. gave birth to several outstanding children, especially Tear Fund, Crusade magazine, the Christian Arts Centre and the Overseas Club for foreign students.

My Presidency gave me immense pleasure and a sense of real satisfaction. I travelled widely with Gordon Landreth whose contribution to the evangelical scene in Britain and Europe has been outstanding. Often we had with us noteable Christian leaders from other parts of the world, such as Luis Palau and Dr. Festo Kevengere.

My Presidency also involved me at a deeper level with evangelicals of other traditions such as the Christian Brethren, Baptists and Methodists. It was not always easy to relate to so wide an understanding of evangelicalism and sometimes I felt as though I was driving a carriage with four horses, each one pulling in a different direction. But I hope I was able to provide evangelicals with some sense of direction. I considered holding this office as one of the highlights of my ministry.

Meanwhile Olive and I were constantly being invited

to return to Latin America to share in some way the expanding life and witness of the Anglican Church there. There was an extra incentive too: John and Jennet were firmly established in Arequipa in Peru and in 1978 Jennet gave birth to our first grandchild, Nicholas.

It was fascinating to compare the situation in the late '70s with that before the Forward Move of the early '60s. Almost unbelievable progress had been made. In 1961 the whole work was dominated by the missionary society for understandable reasons. But now the work was, in many instances, led by national Bishops and Pastors with the missionary society used as more of a backup.

Another huge leap forward from 1961 was that the property and land then belonging to the missionary society now belonged, with just a few exceptions, to the national Church. In 1961 the main thrust of SAMS work had been to the Indian tribes of Chile, Paraguay and Northern Argentina. But now Arthur Goodwin Hudson's vision of work in the towns and cities was a reality. SAMS was established in some of the largest cities in Latin America including Santiago, Temuco and Vina del Mar in Chile; Asuncion and Concepcion in Paraguay; Salta and Buenos Aires in Argentina, Rio de Janeiro and San Salvador in Brazil and Lima and Arequipa in Peru.

Olive and I also could not help noticing the increased breadth of the SAMS ministry. Alongside church planting and evangelism, a high proportion of our staff and resources were directed towards education projects, agricultural schemes, medical programmes and drawing up theological curricula.

The outcome of all this was an improvement of living conditions among those Indians whose plight had so horrified and grieved me on my first visit. Magnificent support from Tear Fund, Christian Aid and Oxfam had enabled SAMS to embark on undreamt-of projects. There have been tremendous strides forward in preventative medicine in Northern Argentina and astounding progress made in the field of agriculture. An immense amount of relief has also been brought to the Indian people of Paraguay and the improved health of the children was abundantly evident. The standard of our hospital at Maquehue near Temuco in South Chile was now second to none elsewhere in the republic. Furthermore, our schools in Asuncion, Paraguay, and Vina del Mar, Chile, could only be described as among the best.

The only visible weakness was the SAMS failure to make inroads at student level in the colleges and universities. An outstanding exception to this was the work of Felicity Houghton who went to Chile with SAMS during the first Forward Move. Her contribution to the university undergraduates of Chile cannot be overrated. She became thoroughly fluent in the Spanish language and had an expert understanding of the Latin American student community. Gradually, and almost entirely due to Felicity, Christian Unions have been established in universities in Chile and in other republics too. The challenges that remain, I believe, are to train Latin Americans to perform this student work themselves, and to encourage them to write their own theological and devotional books.

One overwhelming observation we made on our last official tour of the field was the fine calibre of the SAMS missionaries. Our 150 strong team was, for the most part, made up of fully consecrated, highly skilled operators who were performing a monumental work with only the minimum amount of support from the Church at home. On reflection I could not recall a time when the support matched the quality or quantity of the work in Latin America.

On deputation work I set out to paint as realistic a

picture as I could of the work in Latin America. But somehow I gained for myself the reputation of preaching, 'the truth, the whole truth and a little bit more than the truth!' I grinned and bore what was meant to be a friendly criticism. But I believed what I said – and assure readers of this chapter that I have only told *the truth*!

13: The West End

Something as simple as a knock at the door, a phone call or a letter can often be the means of making one rethink the direction of one's life. And it was a letter in early 1978 that set Olive and I off on an unexpected path. I was three years from retirement and, although God had wonderfully protected me through a further decade of extensive travel, my angina was very painful at times and I tired very quickly. Olive too was increasingly troubled by arthritis. In fact she had reached the stage where she felt she could no longer accompany me on my travels.

The unexpected letter arrived as we were sharing these particular problems with the Lord and seeking His solution. It invited me to succeed Bishop Goodwin Hudson who, on his return from Australia, had become Vicar of St. Paul's, Portman Square, in the West End of London. During his incumbency, the church had, in fact, moved out of Portman Square to Robert Adam Street. The thought of returning to parish life had never really occurred to me after twenty years with SAMS. I had kept in close touch with parish churches but I had forgotten what it was like to have full responsibility for one parish.

It was important that we did not take long in coming to a decision. Every church in the London diocese that becomes vacant has its future very carefully considered by the Pastoral Committee of the diocese, and one or two members of the Committee felt that because the new St. Paul's was so close to All Souls', Langham

Place, a successor to Bishop Goodwin Hudson should *not* be appointed but a different role found for the church.

In view of the perfect timing of this invitation when we were so much in prayer about our future, Olive and I felt this was a call from the Lord. A more settled ministry with less physical demands was attractive; we also believed it presented an opportunity to witness for Christ in the West End of London.

Little did I know when I moved into St. Paul's in October 1978 that the ensuing three years were going to be among the most challenging and difficult of my whole life. Even at my age, with so much abundant evidence of God's constant faithfulness over so many years, I wondered if He *had* led me right. Early on there were times when I was thoroughly perplexed and tended to question God's leading in the matter of returning to parochial life. But God does not make mistakes. Looking back, I realise that my brief and relatively uneventful ministry there served as an important bridge in the life of the church itself. And I learned lessons which have proved invaluable in my retirement.

The new church was undoubtedly the most modern Anglican Church in the West End. Externally, however, the building tended to look more like a hotel and even taxi drivers did not recognise it. One entered St. Paul's through large glass doors and found oneself in a carpeted foyer with a wide staircase beyond. The parish office, vestry and choir room were on this floor. Downstairs was a beautifully appointed restaurant known as the Red Room. Upstairs was the worship area which comfortably seated about 260 people. It was spacious, light and airy with blue and gold colours in pre-eminence. There was a large, well furnished lounge adjacent to it. Above there were eight flats, one of which was the vicarage. In the basement there were garages.

The modern style of architecture had its critics of course. I personally liked it and found a spiritual, worshipful atmosphere was readily created there. My only problem was the pulpit. This, for some reason, was in a lofty position far removed from the congregation. I found this created not just a physical void between the congregation and me, but also an emotional barrier. It was not long before I installed a small lectern on the chancel steps where I felt much more at home.

Our vicarage overlooking Manchester Square Gardens was nothing short of luxurious. But the disadvantage of living so close to the church was the impossibility of getting away from its demands. I have to confess that I had great difficulty in relaxing in such circumstances. I also found it hard to adapt to so much that is taken for granted in parochial life. Although I had been a regular visitor to parish churches during my twenty years with SAMS, I had quite forgotten what it was like to have the sole responsibility for a church and to work with a PCC. Once more I was confronted with the irritations of parish life and, at first, these seemed to outweigh the joys and privileges. It was I who was blamed if the colour of the flowers was not that requested and I who was pressed to hasten changes in the format of our worship.

It did me little good either to refer back to the other twenty years parish experience. St. Paul's, Robert Adam Street, was quite unique. It was certainly totally unlike the Merseyside parishes and the churches in Lowestoft and Blackpool where we had been so abundantly blessed. There, packed Sunday services were the great climax to the week and the festivals were magnificent family occasions with capacity congregations. In contrast the West End of London emptied on a Sunday and we were not sufficiently well known to attract many visitors. All Souls', Langham Place, was within walking distance and, as far as I was concerned, squeezed the sponge dry of visiting worshippers to our part of town. I must hasten to add however that Michael Baughan, then Rector of All Souls', became a fine friend and adviser. To add to my problem, a good half of our congregation were professional people and students who regularly went home at weekends and for holidays. There was an uncanny inactivity on a Sunday and I could not come to terms with it.

It was not until the Sunday services actually started at 11 a.m. or 6.30 p.m. that I realised it was Sunday at all. After about four months struggling to overcome my problems and tending to look in instead of up, I fell into a deep depression the severity of which took me utterly by surprise. I had hoped that by now I would be seeing a numerical response to my ministry but this was not the case and I felt a failure. The large airy church seemed strangely empty with no more than fifty worshippers on an ordinary Sunday morning and seventy at night.

I especially remember my first Easter Sunday morning. I looked out into the street and my heart sank: not even a bird or a cat was stirring! Eventually about eighty people gathered round the Lord's Table to celebrate His resurrection. The evening congregation was a little larger and I was encouraged by a young lady professing to having found Christ that night. Olive gently reminded me that the wonderful fact of Christ's resurrection was no less thrilling or worthy of celebration whether two or three, or two or three thousand had gathered. I knew she was right of course. The fact that Jesus was alive and that I *knew* He was alive in me was the essence of the Easter Sunday message. Numbers were irrelevant. But of course depression plays havoc with fact, with reason and with faith.

Uncharacteristically, I began to worry about all sorts of small details in my life and I had considerable difficulty sleeping. For example, retirement worried me because I was aware that I had no financial resources. I knew perfectly well that the Heavenly Father who had led and provided for us for forty years would not let us down now. But that no longer proved enough.

I must emphasise that, during this time, I never lost touch with God, or perhaps I should say, God never lost touch with me. In fact there would have been those in the congregation who were unaware that anything was wrong. Some knew – and prayed for me. Chief among my comforters was Olive. She was pure gold. One morning while we were having our daily prayer time together, I broke down in tears. Olive took my hand and continued where I had left off. She has never mentioned the episode since. Not once did she lose patience with me, not once did she try to tell me to 'snap out of it' – which is of course the worst possible advice for anyone suffering from depression. Her contribution was one of loving, patient, prayerful support although she herself was often in much pain and physical discomfort. In fact on another morning she quite suddenly collapsed. She looked absolutely terrible and I really feared she had died. She was rushed to the Middlesex Hospital where she was detained for several weeks, apparently suffering from complications with her arthritis.

When she returned home, our daughter Janet kept a watchful eye on us and the congregation at St. Paul's was wonderfully supportive and kind. My own doctor, Maxwell Jones, a great Christian friend as well as physician, helped me to cope with my depression by means of counselling, prayer and medication. I look upon the months from March to July of 1979 as the most difficult period of my life. I really did struggle. I was thankful still to have alongside me at St. Paul's the curate I had 'inherited', Keith Townley. In addition to being an excellent curate Keith Townley turned out to be one of my best friends and his continued friendship is a source of great pleasure to both Olive and myself. Keith had already been at the church for four years but he stayed on and proved a wonderful support and encouragement. It had been made clear to me that when Keith did leave there was no possibility of my having another curate. Nevertheless when the time came for Keith to move on, because Olive was still unwell and I continued to battle against depression, I decided to share my position with a senior member of the diocesan staff.

I must say that in all my forty years in the ministry I have never found a Bishop who has fulfilled the role of 'father in God' to me. I cannot recall one with whom I have felt able to share in any depth. Always I have felt inferior and ill at ease and this occasion did nothing to restore the balance. I was listened to but not heard; the burden of my heart was presented but not understood. Our conversation was interrupted after about a quarter of an hour by the telephone. When he left the room, I distinctly heard my interviewer say, 'Now he knows how the other half lives.' This comment summed up for me how, very sadly, I have constantly found myself quite out of tune with Bishops. Considering my upbringing in working class Liverpool, twenty years' busy and hard experience of parish life and a further twenty years itinerant ministry for SAMS, I felt it was an unkind comment. But it was not the implied criticism that saddened me, it was the complete lack of understanding. I had *not* gone to him seeking sympathy, but I *had* hoped for positive encouragement. I needed help, guidance and support at this particular period of my life when both Olive and I were unwell and were feeling the burden of responsibility for St. Paul's. I terminated the interview as soon as I could and left with a heavy heart.

However, one good thing did come out of my interview. It was agreed that I should have some help in the ministry at St. Paul's. So it was that Andrew Kirk, who was on the staff of SAMS, was invited to help us on a part time basis. Andrew's contribution was outstanding in every way. Friends wondered how we would get on together – Andrew is a scholar and I have few academic qualifications. However, we got on famously and fitted in together perfectly. Andrew Kirk supplied a dimension to the ministry which would have been lacking had I been on my own. The life and witness of St. Paul's was greatly enriched by Andrew Kirk's presence among us.

The depression stayed with me into the summer months. My faith was shaken and tested to its very roots. There were days when all I could manage by way of prayer was to say the name of Jesus. But I proved God to be a God of the valleys as well as the mountain tops. I knew the reality of God in those dark days. My depression never reached the depths of despair because the Lord provided light in the darkness, comfort in the sorrow and encouragement in moments of deepest despondency. 'God is faithful and will not let you be tempted beyond your strength, but with the temptation will also provide the way of escape, that you may be able to endure it.' (1 Corinthians 10: 13)

At last, by the autumn of 1979, I was well on the road to recovery and my ministry began to come alive again. In fact, my ministry began to take on one or two extra dimensions possibly because of my illness. I found I was approached far more often for private advice and counselling. I had never considered myself a good listener but having so recently been through the valley myself, I suppose people felt I could now identify with their problems. I considered this a great privilege and could have given much more time to this particular ministry.

The Sunday congregations stayed about the same size although a few more young people, particularly students and nurses, now joined us regularly. From time to time our evening Holy Communion services were combined with a healing ministry. I remember how glad we were to receive a letter from a doctor in Lancashire telling us how one of his long-term patients, an arthritic, had been cured during a visit to one of our Holy Communion services. The doctor explained that he himself was not a Christian, but he thought we would be encouraged to hear that this patient had now been discharged after several years of suffering. It was a 'medical mystery' for which we praised God!

We were not a large congregation but we were extremely happy and united. Some Sunday evenings, when the Holy Spirit had blessed our worship in a special way, the people were reluctant to leave the church and our fine young organist, David Evans, always found suitable, beautiful music to match the mood of the hour.

The Tuesday evening fellowship flourished. Supper was served first in our church restaurant, and then we met together in house Bible study groups one week and as a whole church fellowship the next. Every fifth Tuesday we made our time together a 'St. Paul's Night', – an occasion for evangelism. A buffet supper was followed by first class entertainment and a short evangelistic address. Many souls were saved on those memorable St. Paul's Nights. On one outstanding Tuesday evening our guest was the then Bishop of Woolwich, Michael Marshall. He is a most accomplished pianist and he provided us with some excellent entertainment before giving a short, but powerful evangelistic address based on Psalm 23. Many were converted that night; Olive and I helped enquirers for well over an hour afterwards.

I continued under constant pressure to make changes in the format of our worship. I was accused by some of maintaining old fashioned services in a modern building. I knew very well that if St. Paul's was to survive, radical changes would have to be made. But my sympathies lay very much with those who had worshipped at the church since its Portman Square days. So many of the professional people and students went home at weekends or holiday times. I liked things as they were – using the 1662 Prayer Book with some degree of flexibility, along with the Anglican Hymn Book.

We occasionally let our hair down however! Once Cliff Richard was our special guest at a Sunday evening service; he sang in his inimitable way and finished, as he often does, by inviting the congregation to join him in singing 'How Great Thou Art', linking hands and raising arms all along the pews. Several of the older members confided afterwards that this was the first time they had ever raised their arms in worship but, in that sort of environment, it had come naturally.

Olive's health improved and she thoroughly enjoyed being involved in the life of a parish once again. It was a long time since Blackpool days and she was back in her element. Her particular responsibility was the midweek fellowship for women on a Wednesday afternoon. About twenty ladies would meet for prayer and Bible study and these were times of fellowship, friendship and blessing. On a Wednesday too we held our midweek service which was preceded by lunch in the church restaurant.

I was conscious of the great potential of our excellent facilities at St. Paul's for Christian outreach apart from our own. Our church administrator Rosa Wright set about a programme of hiring and letting the premises to various Christian organisations. Such missionary societies as SAMS, CPAS and BCMS were among the groups that began to use the church for public rallies. There was, of course, a strong missionary dimension to our own work at St. Paul's. We had an effective missionary committee and we kept in close touch with our personal contacts in India, Thailand, South America and North Africa. We had a regular missionary focus at Evening Prayer when a member of the missionary committee would bring us up to date with news. On our annual missionary gift day, friends from all over the world came to visit us. Our missionary giving quadrupled.

One of the highlights of our time at St. Paul's was when Emmanuel, an African ordinand, worked with us for two months under the auspices of African Enterprise. What a ministry Emmanuel had among us! Every smile he gave us was a benediction. Other young students from Switzerland and Germany also served on our staff for short periods and we had an increasing number of young people worshipping with us from various parts of the world including Australia, Turkey, the United States and Brazil.

So, after the severe problems of the early months, my short ministry at St. Paul's developed into one of joy and fruitfulness. Olive, despite recurring ill health and hospitalisation, was outstandingly happy there. But, as my sixty fifth birthday drew nearer, we began to pray very earnestly about the future. While Olive was receiving first class attention at one hospital, I was always under the watchful eye of the National Heart Hospital where doctors advised me to retire as soon as possible.

One day I received a surprise telephone call. The caller said he was Tony Guest whom I had met very briefly on one or two occasions. Tony said he had felt very strongly during his prayer time that morning that God was directing him to speak to me. I assumed Tony was possibly wanting some sort of counselling and invited him to come and have a chat. We talked fairly generally for the first few minutes, then Tony asked where we intended to live after retirement. I said I did not know but that Olive and I had been making this an urgent matter of prayer. Tony proceeded to explain the real reason for his visit. He had felt prompted to offer us a house! He and his family had moved into a larger house and were in a position to allow us the use of their first property. Our joy was complete when we discovered that this house was 3, Starling Close, in Buckhurst Hill, next door to Woodford Green where we had spent our twenty wonderfully happy years with SAMS. A further lovely 'coincidence' was that the Rector of the parish in which we would be living was Gaunt Hunter, in whose parents' house Olive and I had begun our married life together in Fazakerley. I had also had the privilege of being one of the human instruments in leading Gaunt Hunter to the Saviour.

There was no doubt about it: God had put His seal on our future. Having served a short but strategic ministry in the West End, it was time to retire and to leave a younger man to put into effect the changes I knew were necessary if the church was to have a real identity in the '80s. Now we trusted the Lord to turn us into useful senior citizens!

14: New Beginnings

Friends at St. Paul's had always been kind and generous to us and characteristically they rallied round to help when removal day arrived in September 1981. It poured with rain but all went smoothly and within a few days we were happily settled in our new home in Buckhurst Hill, Essex.

What to do now? We viewed our retirement with mixed feelings. Olive especially regretted having to put behind her the day-to-day involvement of parish life. But we were to discover that days of retirement can be wonderfully fulfilling. Events overtook me at first and, without realising it, I found myself caught up in an absorbing and time consuming role as chairman of the Luis Palau North East Mission to London. I had no idea when I accepted the invitation just what would be involved! Additionally, with plans under way for the 1984 Mission England with Billy Graham, I found myself travelling the length and breadth of the country leading or taking part in evangelistic meetings in preparation for the two missions.

I soon realised I must call a halt and take stock, otherwise my retirement would just become a prolongation of my working life. I asked a young friend from SAMS days who lived in Woodford Green to help me and so, with Chris Wayman's help, I organised my diary and settled down to coping with the huge amount of mail we were receiving. Olive and I always made a careful note of the names and addresses of any who professed faith in Christ through my ministry and we endeavoured to follow them up with a personal letter and a booklet. Within a few months we had over ninety on our list. So, as you can see, retirement was proving not the end, but simply another beginning.

I am convinced that any Christians who are fit and well when they retire, or who are able to retire early, should grasp the opportunity and put it to good use in the service of the Lord. We had a magnificent example of this at St. Paul's, Robert Adam Street in our church administrator, Rosa Wright. Rosa had worshipped at St. Paul's for thirty years and her career had been in the Civil Service. When she retired she transferred all her skill and ability to working for the church in an honorary capacity – sometimes up to sixty hours a week. She was a most invaluable asset. There must be very many churches all over the country that would benefit from the experienced administrative or clerical skills of its retired members. Other retired folk might have a special gift for, say, pastoral visitation which they have been unable to exercise during their working life. I am sure the vast majority of clergy would be only too pleased to welcome such support and would be ready to give any training where necessary.

Another aspect of our retirement that Olive and I especially appreciate is the opportunity every day to have an unhurried time of Bible reading and prayer together. At 8.30 each morning we begin our time of devotion and intercession and we have a growing list of friends who have requested prayer. Many on this list are ill and we remember them in our prayers every day. We pray for their healing but, from experience, we know that God can bless in a very special way in times of illness and through pain when it is committed to Him. We are encouraged when friends write to tell us that they are feeling the benefits of prayer. We hope soon to back up our prayer ministry with a letter and a booklet of encouragement. The ministry of healing is, without doubt, a thoroughly perplexing one. Sometimes it seems our prayers go unanswered and at others they are answered only very slowly. Nevertheless despite the mystery and dilemma, we can confidently testify from our own experience that we can trust in the love and the sovereignty of God in these matters.

We also find that we have additional time at the end of the day, so we have made a point of inviting more people to come and share an evening meal with us. If our friends are not Christians we pray beforehand that we shall have an opportunity to witness for Christ during the course of the evening. If they are Christians, we love to have fellowship with them and to encourage them as we eat and talk together in a relaxed atmosphere.

At the risk of sounding a bit eccentric, I must also add the pleasure it gives me nowadays to have time to chat to the seven goldfish we have in our little garden pool. What a joy it is to have time to 'stand and stare' as well as to have more time for people. The fish make their appearance as I feed them and, although I expect no response, I find it most relaxing to have a little talk to them! On a more serious note, the extra time I have for people enables me to get to know them better and therefore, I trust, to make my conversation more relevant to their situation.

There was a momentous break in life's new pattern in the early weeks of 1982. Thanks to the generosity of many friends at St. Paul's, we were able to travel to Latin America to visit some of the projects with which we had been closely associated in our days at SAMS. Our first stop was at Boys' Town in Rio de Janeiro. When we first shared in this project with Edgar and Amy Nicholls it was pathetically inadequate, but over the years it had become one of the finest. The project was something of a Dr. Barnado effort. Edgar and Amy rescued boys from the streets and sewers of Rio. They extended love and care to the boys, helping them to lead full lives and training them to become useful citizens of Brazil.

At first Edgar and Amy's headquarters were cavelike dwellings but soon the Protestant Episcopal Church of the USA and the Brazilian government, seeing the great value of the SAMS initiative, began to give their support. Then Tear Fund took up the project so that modern buildings and facilities replaced the old premises and Edgar and Amy continued to work for and with the abandoned boys. Little did we know as we said our farewells to the Nicholls that this would be the last time we would see Edgar this side of heaven. He died a few months later from a heart attack. His work at Boys' Town remains a lasting tribute.

We flew next to Southern Chile where we had spent many happy days. A project here close to our hearts was the hospital at Maquehue. Twenty five years ago this was a large wooden structure. Amazing changes had taken place and now this fine hospital was second to none in the whole of Chile. One thing had not changed during the course of time and that was the excellent quality of the SAMS missionary nurses. At the time of our last visit, Jenny Thornton and her staff were maintaining this great tradition.

We moved on to Santiago. The work here had been slow to take root but, by now, the advances had overcome the discouragements. The work was under the leadership of Bishop Colin Bazley, one of our finest missionary Bishops. Colin went to Chile with his wife Barbara and small daughters in 1962 and Olive and I had enjoyed many happy times of fellowship with the Bazley family over the years.

Undoubtedly we would have to say that the highlight of our retirement trip was our visit to Arequipa in Peru. This was a double thrill because, not only were we there to witness a significant event in the life of the national church, but we were to stay with John, Jennet and our two small grandchildren, Nicholas and Rebecca. Bishop David Evans was now heading the work in Peru and we were in Arequipa for the inauguration of the Anglican Church there. On a human level the Church of the Redeemer, Arequipa, was the result of John and Jennet's work. The £30,000 needed for the building had been a gift from our All Saints' Church in Woodford Green. There is a tablet in the entrance of the church recording the date of the inauguration, January 31st, 1982, and the fact that it might never have been opened but for the faithfulness and generosity of the people of All Saints', Woodford Green.

This was possibly the most memorable moment of our lives. We were overcome with emotion when Bishop Evans invited Olive to pray the dedicatory prayer. After the dedication, a national Peruvian Pastor was ordained and our granddaughter Rebecca was baptised. It was a glorious occasion for which our hearts were full of thanksgiving to God. So we returned elated and refreshed ready to take up again the threads of our retirement ministry.

People often ask me, now that I have retired, whether I have any special joys or regrets as I look back over my ministry. On the positive side I would want to praise God that right from the first day of finding Christ as my Saviour, He implanted in my heart the desire to serve Him wholly. Before my conversion I was never half hearted about anything: the church choir, football, scouting – it did not matter what it was. Since the day of my conversion, I have counted it a great honour to give God my time, my energy, my money and whatever gifts I may have. All these were His gift to me in the first place and I very gladly gave them back to use as He saw fit. So, if there has been a plus to my ministry, perhaps it is that I have never been half hearted about anything I have undertaken – not least proclaiming the Gospel.

In the fulfilment of this, of course, I have had the unwavering love and support of Olive for over forty years. I vividly recall the evening in 1935 when I was courting Olive and I told her that I believed God was calling me to full time service. 'If He does,' she replied, 'I can think of no greater pleasure than the prospect of being married to one of God's servants. I will support you in every way I possibly can.' And she has.

Of course, happy marriages do not just happen. I think many Christian marriages start out based on the false assumption that, as it is Christian, it will inevitably be successful. Because of the sinfulness of human nature, this is far from the truth. Marriage requires working at: there is a continuing need to be prepared to give as well as to take. Commitment to Christ provides a genuine basis for confidence and optimism. A key ingredient in our harmonious relationship has been prayer together every day whenever I was at home. In this way a strained atmosphere could not last longer than the next prayer time. If we came to the Lord together in prayer as two individuals with a difference, we came away from our prayer forgiven and united in His love.

I was astonished recently when taking part in a forum at a well known convention in the presence of several thousand people. One of the questions asked was, 'Do members of the panel find it easy or difficult to pray with their respective partner in marriage?' I found myself the only one of the panel who made a common practice of praying with my wife. I just could not understand how Christian folk can deny themselves such blessing! Praying with Olive has been one of the greatest strengths of our marriage and my ministry.

We have always endeavoured to be thoroughly open with each other. We have discussed problems, fears, hidden hopes and aspirations. Our life has been one of total sharing. This principle included our bank account which has always been in our joint names and each of us has always had complete freedom to draw upon the balance. I have to admit however that there was never much in the balance until I reached the age of sixty! But again Olive has never complained: this was part and parcel of the commitment she gave that evening in Arrow Park, Birkenhead. I think some marriages undergo strain because money and 'keeping up with the Joneses' assumes too great a priority. It is essential that a couple should have mutual confidence in each other where money is concerned.

My absence from home for long periods during our children's teenage years meant an added responsibility for Olive. In my view she did a remarkably fine job in that neither Janet nor John ever gave us any major problems and both, in their own way, profess allegiance to Christ. If the pattern of family life had changed a little during a long absence, I never sought to alter it and I made sure I caught up and adapted to the change myself. An example of this was after a long tour of Latin America I returned to find the children watching television on a Sunday. For many years we had endeavoured to keep Sunday free from television. But I was sure Olive had hammered the issue out with the children and her decision to relax the rule was right with me.

It was a great joy for me to return home after any deputation work. Whatever the hour of night or day, Olive would be there to greet me. Even at 2 or 3 a.m. she would be up and dressed with all those things ready that she knew I appreciated at the end of a tiring day. I was thoroughly spoilt with hot water ready for a bath and Coca Cola cool in the fridge! Above all she never asked questions. She let me unwind then, after a good night's sleep, we told each other our news.

One issue with which we needed to come to terms at a

very early stage was Olive's problem of deafness. I have always wanted to protect her on public occasions in particular, but the fine line that exists between helping and interfering was one I often crossed. I shall always remember getting into trouble over this issue at a Bishop's garden party. Knowing that Olive's hearing aid would be picking up all the background noise of a crowded, social occasion, I tried to compensate for her as well as carrying on my own conversation. The Bishop concerned did not know of Olive's problem and accused me of talking too much. Perhaps he was right!

In the end of course our happy and stable relationship rests on one old fashioned quality. Physical attraction and common interests have their part to play in marriage but they are totally inadequate; quite simply we love one another. This true love breeds mutual respect. We have never taken it for granted and never taken each other for granted. In fact, even after all these years, there are still surprises in our marriage. Something I say or do evokes unexpected pleasure or displeasure in Olive which I had not realised before. Such is the adventure of sharing a life completely with another!

In the face of so many blessings, my deepest regret is that I have not always trusted God as implicitly as I should. Looking back I can see that never once has God failed me, but as I have looked forward too often I have tended to falter. How little hearts have changed since the Children of Israel wandered in the wilderness for forty years daily experiencing miracles from God, but daily doubting and questioning Him for the future! I am confident that my guarantee of tomorrow should be seen in the light of yesterday's wonderful faithfulness. I deeply regret the fretting and anxiety over little details which have surely weakened my ministry. As I look forward, I pray that, in my old age, my life may more truly reflect a complete restfulness and confidence in His constant love. I still have much to learn.

On a wider scale my ministry has spanned a significant period in recent history. There were the war and post war years when so many were trying to find themselves again after all the devastation; the 'we've never had it so good' '60s when materialism was rampant, the Beatles reigned and church going declined. Then the growing disillusionment of the '70s and '80s as prosperity and materialism were found not to satisfy.

During this period the Church has had grievous problems adapting to change. We often speak of the Church failing to penetrate the world, but in the late '40s and '50s the world wanted to penetrate the Church and could not because those inside the Church made it so difficult for people to hear and understand the meaning of the Gospel. In the post war era the Archbishop of York, William Temple, produced a document 'Towards the Conversion of England' which, in my view, is still the best statement ever produced concerning what the Church ought to be doing. It was written at a time when people would have been responsive and ready to receive its message but, alas, it was never followed up. Evangelism has often been applauded throughout the Church of England, but rarely applied. The Gospel of the Lord Jesus Christ has not been made available and relevant to the man and woman in the street.

Today, I feel, we have come full circle from those post war days. We are in a similarly questing and responsive climate for the message of the Gospel. After the war people were asking, 'Where do we go from here?' Today we have experienced all the hollow satisfaction that prosperity had to offer and we are asking again, 'Where do we go from here?' Sadly the established Church is again failing to point the way.

Where the traditional church is failing, the House Church Movement has arisen in order to compensate. I am sorry that this movement ever came about for I believe that, in the long term, it will weaken rather than strengthen the Christian cause in Britain. Whenever I have made an excursion into the house church environment I have felt strangely ill at ease. At heart I am a churchman – at home in a building with traditionally ecclesiastical architecture and stained glass windows! Nevertheless I have sympathy for those young Christians who have become increasingly frustrated by the closely knit structures of the traditional church. I see the House Church Movement as a revolt against a lack of opportunity to witness in the world through the established church and as a means to worship in a free, demonstrative way.

Usually, however, a house church has come into being not only as a form of rebellion but because there was a leader or leaders who were ready to take advantage of the situation. Often members of a new house church who broke away from a traditional church because it was too parson orientated, have found themselves with a new kind of parson who dominates the scene to a far greater extent than the old one. This cannot be healthy.

In the first place the House Church Movement grew at the expense of the traditional church. There was little growth – only transfer. Today it is a different story. Many of the house groups are attracting new members in the neighbourhood, which can only be a good thing. Whether the house churches will survive once the charismatic leaders who took them out of the traditional churches have grown old is a matter for debate. My own view is that they have come to stay and they will continue to meet the needs of those who desire an expressive form of worship with plenty of structural outlets for them to use in their service for God. I would prefer to see the traditional churches learning some lessons from the Movement. There is an urgent need for lay people to have more scope to serve God within and through the established church. If this need is met, then some of the causes that make the House Church Movement necessary will be removed.

However, there *has* been healthy progress towards democratisation of the Church. I recall my old Vicar in Toxteth, Canon Copner, still bemoaning the inauguration of Parochial Church Councils as a device of the devil! He much preferred the old vestry meeting of the Vicar and two church wardens! We have at least come some way forward since those bad old days. Regrettably there are reversals scattered along the way. Recent teaching by some Bishops that a clergyman in the Church of England, when he takes Holy Communion, does so on behalf of the Bishop in his absence, leaves me totally baffled. Such a concept in my opinion is complete gobbledegook and is totally unrelated to Bible teaching.

I must add too how significantly the clergyman's lot has improved since I started out on my ministry. A curate today is infinitely better off and, at the other end of the scale, the retired clergyman is far better provided for. There are still inequalities however and I hope these will continue to be ironed out.

Thankfully these forty years have seen a diminution in the confrontation between the Anglo-Catholic and Evangelical elements within the Church of England. We have learned to understand each other better and to tolerate each other, although there are still great theological barriers between us.

One of my deepest regrets as I survey the Christian scene is that I too often sense a lack of real commitment to Christ among those who call themselves Christians. This goes hand in hand with a decline in moral standards. Attitudes to sex, to marriage, to money and to pleasure are often lax. Frederick P. Wood's book 'Doubtful Amusements' which so influenced me as a young Christian would be poles apart from most young

Christians today. As a result, their witness is vague and ineffectual. The Cross of our Lord Jesus Christ is used as a raft on which to float comfortably along with the tide of the times, rather than as an object of sacrificial commitment. Christian people need to spend more of their time at Calvary and to examine their lives in the light of the Saviour's sacrifice. Evangelical Christians so often lack authenticity and one crucial reason is that they tolerate and excuse sin in their lives. Sin must not be allowed to have subtle dominion over us. The power of sin needs to be overcome daily at the foot of the Cross in penitence.

Then, as a consequence, I should love to see a return to the position among evangelicals where the winning of souls for Christ is considered a real priority. While I accept that revival is the sovereign act of God and that the initiative lies with Him, I believe there is a vital link between God's sovereignty and man's responsibility. There has never been a revival since the day of Pentecost that has not arisen out of a group of praying believers.

So many of us in the middle of very busy lives applaud and acknowledge the importance of prayer but we must accept that we need discipline in order to apply it. Thinking about a good meal does not satisfy our hunger; in the same way thinking about prayer does nothing to satisfy our soul and will supply no spiritual nourishment whatsoever. Over the years I have become increasingly aware that prayer is the major requisite for any individual or corporate undertaking for Christ if it is to have any impact.

In this age of compromise there is a need for Christians to be honest with God. His power cannot be released in us while we are harbouring sin, fear or despondency in a dark corner of our lives. I do not think we should always expect the sensational from God, but I *do* believe we should be prepared to see Him at work in our lives every day. The old hymns and choruses have passed out of fashion nowadays, but their somewhat quaint wording takes some beating. If only we could really grasp hold of this one:

> In my heart the Saviour lives,
> Victory over sin He gives.
> By His wondrous grace divine
> Resurrection life is mine!

I have to confess there have been moments when I have doubted the very message I have been called to proclaim simply because it just did not seem to work. In the local church situation the disagreements, tensions, the lack of fellowship and falling out, the ease with which many Christians could lose their temper or fall away from the faith, my own inner thoughts and feelings were all bewilderingly inconsistent with the Gospel. At moments of particular tiredness or pressure all these things combined to prompt me to ask, 'Does what I am saying really work in the lives of ordinary men and women?'

If I shared these doubts with my friends, I did not always find the answer in doing what they recommended which was to fix my eyes on Jesus and not on the people about me. I understood exactly what they meant but this remedy only served to make the situation more perplexing. The whole purpose of my life and ministry was to enable others to be like Jesus and when, after years of Bible reading, church going and professing the Christian faith, their life style was still a long way from that of the Saviour, I was left with the question, '*Does* this really work?'

Invariably God solved the problem for me. He would draw my attention to some delightful Christian person, family or group who exemplified Christian living. The very light of heaven shone through their lives. Their secret was that they were in daily communion with Christ.

Is there any one, however mature a Christian, who has not at some stage in their life sighed with the Psalmist, 'What is man that Thou art mindful of him?' I have certainly had my times of doubting God in the heat of the moment. National, domestic or personal problems have crowded in, circumstances have worked out in an unexpected way and I have found it difficult to believe that God is in control. But one of the great advantages of being retired is that I have time to look back and take stock. In doing so I can now very clearly see the hand of God at work even in those circumstances which at the time seemed inexplicable. From the vantage point of advancing years I can see the picture more completely and I can testify with confidence, 'In everything God works for good with those who love Him, who are called according to His purpose.' (Romans 8:28.)

It is all summed up for me in the song still sung by Liverpool's Kop – 'You'll never walk alone.' Since giving my life to Christ I never have – He has blessed me with the constant companionship of the most wonderful family and friends. But, above all, *He* has been with me always, in good times and in bad. I wholeheartedly recommend Him and would wish the last words of my book to be . . . Thank You Lord.